THE KERYGMA

Caves and shantytown where the Neocatechumenal Way was born (Palomeras Alto, Madrid)

KIKO ARGÜELLO

THE KERYGMA
In the Shantytown with the Poor
An Experience of the New Evangelization:
The *Missio ad Gentes*

~

With contributions by

Antonio Cardinal Cañizares Llovera

Christoph Cardinal Schönborn

*Translated by the
East Coast Neocatechumenal Center, USA*

IGNATIUS PRESS   SAN FRANCISCO

Original Spanish edition:
El Kerigma: En las chabolas con los pobres
© 2012 by Buenas Letras, Madrid

Cover photograph by Palomeras Altas, Madrid

Cover design by John Herreid

© 2014 by Kiko Argüello
Published in 2014 by Ignatius Press, San Francisco
ISBN 978-1-58617-860-4
Library of Congress Control Number 2013916529
Printed in the United States of America ∞

CONTENTS

PREFACE

I have written this little book at the suggestion of Cardinal Cañizares, who thought it important that I say something about what the Lord has done with us in the shantytown with the poor and also that I publish a kerygma that may help the Synod on the New Evangelization, above all through its content and anthropology.

All royalties from this book will be used to help the *missio ad gentes* in the New Evangelization.

KIKO ARGÜELLO

INTRODUCTION

Antonio Cardinal Cañizares Llovera

We were offered this little book on the threshold of the Year of Faith and the Synod of Bishops on the transmission of faith, or rather on an urgent, pressing, and new evangelization. It is a true gift of God, that encourages us and nourishes our faith, dispels our fears, and fills us with the courage to follow its announcement—kerygma—and go out and be valiant witnesses and messengers convinced of the gospel.

This is one of those books that, in its simplicity, is full of substance and depth and it deserves to be read. The book does not leave one indifferent; rather one feels captivated and questioned; it is provoking and moving. I would almost prefer to finish the introduction at this point, because I am tempted to be the "mute guide", who signals with his finger, "It's right there." But I could not resign myself to that, because this book collects and offers something so alive and vital: the announcement of the Kerygma. This announcement is delivered here, just as it was delivered in the moment, with all the strength and ardor of someone who feels the gospel is like a fire in his heart, by Kiko Argüello, founder and initiator of the Neocatechumenal Way: a man whose passion is Christ and to bring Christ to all peoples, so that they can be converted and follow Jesus.

Reading and rereading this book and having heard it time and again in person as a living work, I feel, at the same time, the current weakness in the announcement of the gospel that the earth is asking for, the way dry earth longs for water. It is important that we recognize the weakness and frailty of our faith with sincerity and humility. I believe that in this way we are set in motion and renewed. We need that profound renewal; we need a strengthening of our experience of God and Jesus Christ in order to announce the gospel; we need to welcome the gospel of Jesus Christ again, so that it may become alive in us, so that we may live through him, as the just man lives through faith. In this way and only in this way can we evangelize and attract the nonbelievers and those who are far away.

The world needs the gospel. It needs Jesus Christ. We cannot remain impassive before this need: the biggest need imaginable. This need, not always conscious but still genuine, reaches us like a cry, perhaps not even formulated, from those who have distanced themselves from the faith, from those who do not believe, from those who suffer the destruction of humanity or the emptiness of meaninglessness, from those who suffer indifference and injustice, or from those whose needs and laments are forgotten or avoided by everyone. A cry and a supplication is calling to us Christians, weak as we are, saying, "Help us!"

We live in hard times. We easily complain about them. With an astounding ease we look for someone to blame and believe that nothing can be done to change the difficult situation that we are facing. Typically, we live in a pagan society. In times like these what is at stake is the way we understand life; with God or without God; with hope in eternal life or without a horizon that extends past the goods of this world; with an objective morality, solid and valid for everyone, or with the supreme affirmation of one's liberty as an absolute behavioral norm, to the point that external rules of play apply. And this is very important. One outlook is not the same as the other. This is the challenge for us Christians: that men understand and live their life with God, with Jesus Christ, and with faith in eternal life; that men believe in Jesus Christ, follow him, and reach happiness with him: the truth that makes us free, the love that makes us brothers and sisters.

Christians are not mere spectators. We cannot just sit back and relax or muzzle what we have received. We cannot let the immense wealth of the gospel die—it is an immense wealth, a prized and precious "treasure". We feel the urge to evangelize. We cannot be silent. But we can speak only if we believe: "I believed, therefore I spoke."

We have to start over. We have to begin to evangelize again. We must live and announce the gospel in its most radical and original form and in its basic and fundamental content; its call to conversion. To announce the gospel, as if it had never been heard before, in our houses and our homes, to our neighbors, to those with whom we deal and live, to those with whom we work or study or share our dreams just as it was at the beginning of the Church. As if it were the first time that Jesus Christ were announced in a town, with all the strength of novelty and scandal and all its unmatched attractiveness, without complexes or fears, with an eager simplicity and vigorous enthusiasm, with apostolic audacity, with immense love toward everyone. And that announcement, starting from the joyous experience of faith transforms us from within and makes us live with total confidence and hope in God, who loves us.

We live in an unabashedly pagan environment that influences even those who are baptized—much more so than we realize. We have to learn to live as Christians in this environment. Being the leaven in the dough, like the soul in the body, giving life and breath, fermenting our world. And living as Christians with all that it entails is to live the authenticity of the gospel to the core, to give witness to him, to announce him, to be as the soul is for the body. This should be our answer when facing the lack of evangelization, of the announcement of our Christ to those who do not believe or who are far away from the faith. With the help of God this is possible.

He himself, in our time, raises up people who with "new ardor, new methods, and new expressions" bring the gospel to the peoples. This is what the author of this book, Kiko Argüello does, along with the Neocatechumenal Way that he promotes and inspires and which is approved and encouraged by the Church.

The Neocatechumenal Way is a gift of the Holy Spirit for the Church in the postconciliar age as a way or itinerary for Christian initiation or re-initiation and as an instrument to promote a new and vigorous evangelization. Let us give thanks to God for the great marvels that he is doing on behalf of his Church and of humanity through this Way, for the great blessings and fruits through which God is pouring out upon us through this Way: fruits of conversion; of Christian life; of vocations to the priestly ministry, to the consecrated life, to the missionary action of the Church; fruits of charity, of life lived according to the beatitudes, of generous selflessness, of families that are renewed and open to life. . . . Thank God for this book, that somehow also shows and reflects the face of the

Neocatechumenal Way in one of its basic elements: that of the announcement of the Kerygma for conversion and thanks to its author, who through these pages speaks to each one of the readers with all the strength and freshness of the gospel so that, once our ears are opened to the Word, we may receive him and follow him, without fear and with all the joy of someone who has found an immense treasure.

ANTONIO CARDINAL CAÑIZARES LLOVERA
Prefect of the Congregation for Divine Worship and the Discipline of the Sacraments
November 2012

IN THE SHANTYTOWN

The Witness of
Kiko Argüello

THE CLOSED HEAVENS
AND A LIGHT ON THE HORIZON

Kiko Argüello in Joaquin's shack. In the background can be seen a face of Christ drawn by Kiko.

I'll introduce myself: I am Spanish, born in León in an upper middle-class family. I am the eldest of four children. My father was a lawyer; my maternal grandfather was English. I lived in León for only two years. Afterward, my father was transferred to Madrid and we moved to the capital. The Lord has given me the gift of being a painter. Ever since I was a little boy, everybody appreciated my talent for drawing. Later I studied at the Academy of Fine Arts of San Fernando in Madrid.

My parents were Catholic. My mother was a daily Mass-goer; my father went on Sundays. But as soon as I started studying Fine Arts I found myself in a different environment. It was during the time of Franco and almost everyone there was leftist. Thanks to a group with whom I did theater, I encountered the theatrical works of Jean-Paul Sartre. I remember one of his works titled *No Exit* (*Huis clos*), in which Sartre says that hell is other people and presents a scene in which the characters are condemned to contemplate their defects eternally. In the end, in Jean Paul Sartre I found an answer: everything is absurd. There was an answer. Because I would ask myself "Does God really exist?"

But why did I doubt God? Because, in the end, in my house, the witness of my parents had not been enough and neither was the witness of the environment in which I lived. So God allowed me to undergo a *kenosis*, let's say, a profound descent. I also came to know the thought of other existentialists, Albert Camus, for example, and I found an answer in the absurd. I thought that I shouldn't fool myself: and what if God did not exist? I tried to live like that, seriously: "God does not exist." Heaven was closed for me; it was as if an enormous slab of cement formed on top of me, and life began to be very hard. In essence Sartre was saying, "There was a time when we didn't exist; today we exist; and tomorrow we will cease to exist. We have to accept life like this, accept this reality. We don't have to invent any heaven or anything outside this world, but we have to take into account the reality of existence as it is, that is to say, there is nothing."

I tried to live like this, but soon I realized that when life becomes unbearable there is only one exit: suicide. They say that in the world every second a person commits suicide. In Spain suicide is the most common cause of death; next is cancer, accidents, and so on. All over Europe suicide rates are increasing more and more.

At this time [1959], I was awarded the Premio Extraordinario Nacional de Pintura (National Extraordinary Prize for Painting) (it was even mentioned on television and in the papers). I was surprised at that, but deep down, the prize didn't really solve the problem I had inside. Already in the morning, when I awoke I would ask myself, "To live, for what? To make money? To be happy? What for?" I had money, I had fame, and I wasn't happy; I felt dead inside. Consequently I understood that, if I kept on this track I would end up killing myself.

In this *kenosis*, in this closed heaven, God had mercy on me. I would ask myself "How do people live? How do people manage?" I would see normal people and think: "Don't they ask themselves: Who am I? Who has created me? What is life? Could it be that people don't care about these questions? Maybe the problem is me, that I am a narcissist, a strange person?" I felt as though I had a wet blanket over me that made me continually search for the truth: Who are we and what are we doing in this world? I couldn't be indifferent to whether God exists or not; it was a matter of life and death.

In that situation, in the midst of darkness in which nothing satisfied me, in which everything had turned into ashes—even art, sex, and the rest—in which nothing motivated me, there was a ray of light. I read Bergson, a philosopher of Jewish origin, who wrote, "Intuition is a means toward the knowledge of truth superior even to reason." I thought, what if Bergson is right? I understood that, deep down, I was too rational. That is to say, yes, as an artist, I would ask my intuition if it agreed with the absurdity of existence, and I found that something inside me did not agree: beauty, art, water, flowers, trees. . . . Something was not clicking!

This is how God began to appear on the horizon, it was a faint light, like hope. Following that light, in a tragic moment of my existence I went into my room, I closed the door and I yelled at God: "If you exist, come and help me, because death is in front of me!" Perhaps God permitted this *kenosis*, this descent, this emptying of myself, to make me humble, to make me capable of crying out, of asking for help. And in that moment I encountered something. Because I was asking myself, "What can prove to me that God exists?" the proofs of St. Thomas of Aquinas (there is no watch without a watchmaker, and so on) were not helpful to me. Neither was creation or nature. All of this is very curious. How could I be sure?

~

FROM DEATH TO LIFE: "GOD EXISTS!"

The cave of Basilio, a gypsy who was baptized in the community of the shantytown.

I was studying Fine Arts and in my class there was a priest, also a painter, so I went to speak to him about this. Everything he said seemed to me to be inconsistent. I quickly understood that the problem was faith. I could not give it to myself. So I turned to the Lord in that moment, crying out and all of a sudden I felt inside me the certainty that God existed! I did not feel it as a thought or some kind of reasoning or as a theory. God existed: it was like a touch of substance.

St. Paul says that the Spirit of Christ descends upon a man and bears witness to his spirit that God exists. This is what happened to me; I felt inside that God is there: he exists! God exists! I remember that I began to cry, and I did not understand why so many tears ran down my face: "Why am I crying?" I was crying because deep down I was like a man condemned to death who is supposed to be killed; but at the moment when he is about to be executed he is told that he is free. Because, if God exists, then I exist. I went from death to life: God exists. I felt it inside me as a testimony, as a touch of substance: the divine substance touched my spirit. God exists!

After this encounter I went to look for a priest and I told him, "Father, I want to be a Christian." He asked me, "Are you not baptized?"

I answered, "Yes, I am baptized."

"Have you received your First Communion?"

"Yes."

"So do you need to go to confession?"

"Not right now", I replied.

I realized that my First Communion suit and those catecheses given to me in school were not enough. At a certain time, when I was about sixteen or so, I got rid of all that, because, like my First Communion suit, it had become too tight; it was too small on me. I took it off! I said to the priest, "I want formation, I want to be a Christian." But he did not know what to do with me. There was not—there is not—a school for Christians in the parishes: but what if a philosopher, or an atheist wants to be educated in the faith?

Not knowing what to do with me, he thought of sending me to *Cursillos de Cristiandad.* I went to the *Cursillos* and the leaders helped me; they took away a lot of the prejudices that I had toward the Church, the Vatican, parishes and priests. . . . Prejudices that came from my Marxist friends who could not stand institutions, and so forth—all those ideas that the Left has and especially the Spanish Left.

I was not a Marxist because I used to tell my friends who had a great desire for justice: "I do not understand. You want to create a communist paradise in which there is justice for everyone. But, if you don't have an answer to the rest of history, in the end you are just bourgeois. And what's more: when you will have created that paradise, I'd like to go there with a bomb, because you do not have the right to be happy at the expense of all the injustices of history. You don't know how to make justice for the Africans who were seized and put on ships and who died there like wretches. I feel that my desire for justice is total: either for everyone or for no one. It's absurd that there can be justice for some and not for others: they died and there is no other life; there is nothing. They went through a life of misery, of slavery; they died and there was no answer for any of them." These and other ideas saved me from Marxism.

In the *Cursillos* they invited me to be a catechist, a teacher. I went to the *Cursillo* school and I began to give *Cursillos de Cristiandad*. I went to give the first *Cursillo* in Ceuta and then also in Cáceres, among others.

At the same time my painting changed: I was painting in a very modern fashion and I began to do religious paintings. With some other artists, we formed a group to try to introduce art in church buildings, to make religious art more integrated. At that time, since we were doing sacred art and since we were successful, the Ministry of Culture asked us to put on a very important exhibition in

Madrid. Then the Ministry invited me to represent Spain in an international exhibition of sacred art in France, in Royan.

The Juan March Foundation had given a grant to a Dominican theologian for him to look for meeting points between Protestant art and Catholic art, in accord with the Second Vatican Council. I was invited to go with him, together with a Basque architect and a professional Catalan photographer. I say this because that trip was very important for me, because it put me in touch with the renewal of liturgical art of Germany, France, and other countries. We went to study the architecture of Le Corbusier in France and of Eero Saarinen and of Alvar Aalto in Finland, and we had contact with the Orthodox Church, with the Protestants, and so on.

Before beginning the trip, since the Dominican theologian knew the Little Brothers of Jesus, inspired by Charles de Foucauld, he said to me, "Kiko, before going on this trip, which will be very tiring because we'll have to go through a lot of countries, I would like to invite you to go to the Monegros Desert, in Farlete, in the province of Zaragoza where the Brothers are." We went and we stayed there in retreat for a week, getting ready for the trip. In that desert, which is beautiful and has various caves, there was Fr. René Voillaume, founder of the Little Brothers of Foucauld, with many consecrated men from all over Europe.

I remember that I was there three days in the "Cave of St. Caprasio" fasting. There I came to know the life of Charles de Foucauld. I spoke with Fr. Voillaume, and I was very impressed with the hidden life of the Holy Family of Nazareth and the great love Charles de Foucauld had for the Real Presence of Christ. In Tamanrasset (Algeria) he would spend hours alone in front of the Blessed Sacrament.

~

THE SUFFERING
OF THE INNOCENTS

*A woman with her children looking at her shack after it was
destroyed by the police.*

Upon my return from the trip which turned out to be a very serious and important one for me, I had another encounter with the Lord. (I am relating what God has done with my life in order to describe how he led me to the Neocatechumenal Way.) I shared an artist's studio with another painter and a sculptor. I lived there. I would go to my parents' house to spend Christmas Eve with them. One year, on Christmas day, I went to the kitchen and I saw that the maid who worked for my parents was crying. I asked her what was wrong, and she replied telling me a story that left me dumbfounded. Her husband was an alcoholic; when he would come home drunk, he would hit her and her children with a stick, or he would threaten them with a knife. They had many children and the eldest son would argue back at him. She was terrorized thinking that at any moment they were going to kill each other.

That poor woman started telling me these monstrosities as she cried without stopping. Her life was hell. I asked her, "How can I help?"

She answered me: "Come, please, and speak to my husband!" I went to speak to him, but I soon realized that he was a very difficult person.

After speaking to this man I brought him to the *Cursillos*, where I was a catechist. He saw me preach, and he was impressed, to the point that for a time he quit drinking. But since he was an alcoholic, after a while he went back to drinking, and in that house the tragedies began all over again. That woman did not know to whom to look so she would call me: she would ask me to go there because her son was threatening to kill his father. I went running once, twice, three times. . . .

I understood that I could not go on like that and I thought "What if God is telling me that I have to go live with that family to help that man stop drinking and to save those children who are suffering so much?" That's precisely what I did: I left everything and I went to live there. That woman lived in a frightful neighborhood! Not in the shantytown where the Way was born, but in another neighborhood that had been built after the Civil War, full of poor people overcrowded in tenements where everyone had a tiny kitchen. I slept in the kitchen with the cats. In that environment the Lord was waiting for me.

Sartre says, "Woe to the man whom the finger of God crushes against the wall!" I found many people there who were "crushed against the wall" and I felt overwhelmed. There was a woman who lived nearby, all dressed in black, who had Parkinson's. Her husband had left her. She had a son who was mentally retarded and every day when he came home he would hit her with a stick. I would say, "How horrible! How is this possible? Why her and not me?" I met other people who had been abused as children. This environment was like a descent into the hell of the social catacombs.

I had found myself in front of a human suffering that was unheard of, a sort of Auschwitz. They say that after Auschwitz you can no longer believe in God. . . . Well, despite this I found a surprising answer in this environment: I found myself confronted with the mystery of Christ crucified. I understood that there is a presence of Christ in those who suffer, especially in the suffering of the innocent. There are people who are innocent and who are carrying the sins of others, that horrible sin of the alcoholic, of one who hits his mother, of a retarded son, of incest, for example. By means of this suffering, with Christ those people are bringing salvation to the world.

There is a Real Presence of Christ in the Eucharist, but I thought that the suffering of those innocent people was also a real presence of Christ. That impressed me so much that when I had to do military service in Africa, I was already very restless. God was calling me to him and I thought "I cannot go on like this. If Christ comes tomorrow, in his Second Coming, I would like him to find me at the feet of Christ crucified in those who suffer, with the last ones, crushed against the wall. I wanted to be with them there in adoration on my knees." This feeling was so strong in me that I left everything and went to live among the poor.

~

A CATECHETICAL SYNTHESIS BEGINS

Carmen Hernández in Jerusalem, before meeting Kiko in the shantytown.

I was involved in a group who were trying to help young boys who would sell themselves to homosexuals and to aid prostitutes, and so on. I had a friend who was a social worker working in the shantytown of Palomeras and I told him, "I would like to leave everything and go to live with the poor." He pointed out a place for me: a small valley, full of caves where there were gypsies, *quinquis* [a type of down-and-out who lived with the gypsies], vagabonds, beggars, paupers, old prostitutes —a horrible area. He said to me, "You see that shack of moldy planks? A family lived there but they abandoned it. Kick the door open and you can stay there."

I went to live there with a guitar and a Bible. There was a mattress on the floor. I remember that it was freezing cold. Dogs used to shelter in that shack and the dogs would keep me warm. I would sleep with four or five dogs on top of me; otherwise, I would die of the cold. Afterward, those dogs followed me everywhere. I would move and the dogs would follow me. It was impressive how they followed me.

I used to give classes as an art teacher in a school that was a bit further away, far from the shantytown and I would always arrive late because my shack was chaos. Once one of my neighbors brought me a brazier because it was five degrees below zero.

The neighbors used to ask themselves who I was. I had a beard. I don't know what they must have thought. My shack was close to a road through which gypsies would pass on their way to get water from the fountain that was further up, among the houses of Palomeras Altas. In the shack I had hung a cross. One time a *quinqui* came in, saw the guitar, and we began to speak. He asked me, "What does Jesus Christ say about fighting against your enemy?"

God brought me to that environment, because I would honestly never have gone myself. I didn't go there to teach, even though they were almost all illiterate, nor did I go as a social worker. Absolutely not. I considered them to be Jesus Christ and myself to be a poor sinner who was not worthy to live there, in the midst of that horror of innocents suffering, of the victims of the sins of the others. I felt unworthy, unworthy . . . But the Lord obliged me to find a catechetical synthesis, a way of preaching in that environment, because the people wanted me to speak to them of Jesus Christ.

I told that *quinqui*, for example, that Christ says to love the enemy. He had been at a correctional facility. He had escaped and now he was married and had a number of children. He belonged to a clan of *quinquis* that, like gypsies, had their own structure and laws. In the correctional institution he had learned to read and write. The facility was run by religious who made them go to Mass, pray the Rosary, and so forth, for that reason he had some rudimentary religious understanding. Since he knew how to read, I gave him *The Little Flowers of St. Francis*. He was the head of the clan. He was very impressed reading about St. Francis and we became friends.

He was so impressed by what I would tell him about Jesus Christ that he wanted me to convert the whole clan. He would always insist and tell me, "Come to my house!" and he would take me with him. I remember one time he brought me to a cave that was all dark, full of gypsies and *quinquis*. You couldn't see anything. He told me, "Speak to them of Jesus Christ!"

"Me?"

"Yes. Speak of Jesus Christ."

"But I don't know how to speak of him! What do you want me to say? The *Cursillo* catechesis?"

The gypsies didn't know how to read or write. If you speak to them in abstract terms they won't listen; they won't follow. How do you speak to illiterate gypsies that don't know anything about God? How is it possible? But he was forcing me to speak. I asked myself "How would the Apostles have spoken? How did the Apostles preach?" In the cave there were a lot of gypsy women, those who wear large colorful skirts and beg on the streets, who sell things, and so on. I started to speak of Adam and Eve or something of that sort. A woman in the back got up and said to me, "Have you seen him?" she was the mother of the leader. And the leader said, "Mama! Shut up; be quiet!" but the woman continued, "Have you ever seen a dead man who has come back from the cemetery? I only know of one thing: that my father died, and he has never come back to my house. There must be 'a hand' in heaven, but I don't believe in priests or anything of that sort. If you have seen a dead man who has come back from the grave, I'll listen. If not, I'm done! Let's go!" And all the women got up and the meeting ended.

That woman taught me a lot, because in that moment—since that *quinqui* wanted me to speak about Jesus Christ—I was asking myself how the Apostles preached. I would read Scriptures every day and I had found an episode in the Acts of the Apostles in which Governor Festus told King Agrippa that he had a prisoner who is very interesting. He said that he would like for King Agrippa to listen to him because he was accused of speaking about a dead man that lives, one Jesus, who was dead, but whom Paul asserted to be alive (see

Acts 25:14–19). In this text I understood that from all the conversations that Festus had with Paul, the only thing that that pagan had understood was that Paul spoke of a dead man who had come back from the grave. And that woman had told me that the only thing that she would have agreed to listen to was exactly whether or not I had seen a man raised from the dead, something that would show that after death there is life; that would really prove it. "Have you seen a risen man? If not, I won't listen to you. I don't want sermons."

The Lord began to give us a little bit of the rudiments of the Kerygma. That is to say, the Lord forced us through the poor to find that which afterward became the catechesis that we now give in the parishes.

~

THE RENEWAL OF THE CHURCH THROUGH THE POOR

Manolo and Juliana, a brother and sister of the community of the shantytown.

Another day that *quinqui* called me and said, "Come, let's go out. I have called all the men." All the gypsies were outside sitting on the ground. My shack was in a field on the edge of the desert of Castilla, as I recall, and there in the field about thirty gypsies were sitting on the ground cross-legged. "Come, speak to them of Christ, speak to them of God."

"But I don't know how to speak about God; what do you want me to tell you?"

"Come, come, speak to them as you speak to me."

So I asked a gypsy with very dark skin, "Do you believe in God?" And he said, "Yes."

"Oh, but have you seen him?"

"No."

"So then why do you believe in God? Did your father tell you about him?"

"No."

"Have you ever been to school?"

"No."

"Well, then why do you believe in God? Have you seen him? What color is he? Blue? What is he like?"

He stayed silent.

"You believe in God. Why do you believe in him?" and the gypsy, who was one of those who go through the towns with a cart and fix things (they earn a living like this because they are nomads) told a story. He said, "One time I was in my wagon. I was already married and had a son. I stopped the wagon and looked for a place to eat and rest, and I was under a tree. In that moment the sky went dark and all of a sudden a bolt of lightning fell on my wagon. I was with my wife. We were sitting down. The lightning fell on the wagon and it went up in flames. And my son was inside!" The gypsies believe that in the heavens there is a powerful arm. In that moment he went down on his knees and said to God, "O God, save my son! If you save my son, I promise that my whole life will be for you!" First he said this prayer. Then he went to the wagon that was on fire and the little boy was alive, unharmed and laughing. In that moment he had such a strong experience of the divine, so numinous, that it gave him the certainty: "God exists. No matter who tries to make me believe that God does not exist, I know that he exists."

That man told the story of a concrete event in which he had seen the presence of the divine. The Bible speaks of events; events in which God intervenes: God chooses people and through his interventions, God reveals himself. That is why one of the catecheses that we do in the parishes begins by asking: "Do you believe in God? Why do you believe in God? Do you have an event in your history in which God has intervened or have you only heard of him through hearsay? Tell us about a concrete event of your life." That catechesis was conceived by the gypsies, the poor.

John XXIII, before the Council, said that the renewal of the Church would come through the poor. I can say that in the Way this has been fulfilled.

That *quinqui*, the head of his clan, came one day to speak with me because he was arguing with the leader of another clan (those clans are always fighting with each other, one tribe against another, and in one of those fights, they injured the head of the mother of the other clan's leader and she needed twenty stitches). The *quinquis* and the gypsies lived following the law of *talion*: if you have hit me and they have had to give me twenty stitches, I have to hit you back in the head so that they also have to give you twenty stitches; that was the law among these people.

The two clan bosses had decided to settle the question with a fight between themselves, and the day on which they were going to fight each other was approaching. They had challenged each other to a duel with staffs. The gypsies carry a big stick that ends in a metal cylinder as a weapon. If they hit you with it, they kill you, if they hit you on the head, they break it open. It was going to be a fight to death between the two. That *quinqui* had come to speak to me, and I told him, "Don't go!" But he insisted that he had to go. I read the Sermon on the Mount to him that says; "Do not resist one who is evil" (see Mt 5:39). He told me, "What? If I don't resist evil that guy's going to kill me!"

"Well, let's do something: go, but without a weapon and say to him: hit me if you want."

"But Kiko . . . !"

"You believe in the gospel", I said to that *quinqui*.

And he replied, "Yes. What do I have to do?"

"Go without a weapon, only in this way will you save your life. In the meantime, I will pray." This really happened.

He didn't want to tell me the location of the fight because he didn't want me to go. I only told him that during it I would pray the Rosary. I started to pray it with my arms outstretched thinking: "Where are these guys? Who knows if he's already dead." And while I was praying, I heard the sound of a motorcycle, and I saw that the two of them were coming on it: "All right then, I'll see you later!" And they gave each other a hug.

"What a miracle! What happened?" I asked.

"Look, Kiko, I cheated." And he started telling me how he presented himself at the bar—in the outskirts of Madrid it was little like in the Wild West—where they had agreed to meet and how he had gone without his weapon; he had left it hidden outside. The other one, who was also terrified, when he saw that he showed up without a weapon, started to speak and in the end they decided to resolve the question with money: "if you give me this much money, the matter is resolved." He paid him and they continue being friends. Then we went together to pick up the weapon where he had hidden it.

~

T HE DOGS

Kiko with Antonia, Joaquin's wife, and one of the dogs that used to follow Kiko.

One time I arrived late to the school where I was giving classes and the principal of the school had to get a substitute for me. In front of my students, who were children between ten and eleven years old, to whom I would speak of Christ and who loved me very much, the principal scolded me strongly and told me that he was tired of my arriving late. But I didn't know what to do, because all kinds of things were going on in my shack. One time two guys showed up; one was bleeding after a fight. They were afraid of the police and wanted me to hide them. They continued living with me. They had already been to prison three times. There was also another one: a neighbor of mine who had found a young drunk lost on the street. And what did he do? The only thing he could think of was to bring him to my place! And when I arrived to go to sleep I find this guy on my mattress. "And who is this guy?"

And my neighbor says, "Some poor guy. I found him freezing to death. Where can I send him? And I thought, I know! I'll bring him to Kiko, the divine Kiko (that's how he called me: 'the divine Kiko')!" and from then on that kid didn't leave. He continued living with me. Then there was another one, whose name was Manolo, who begged for alms in the metro. He had polio and went around with crutches. Then came Domingo, a shepherd that

Carmen had met in the La Fortuna barrio, which was full of rag and bone men. He worked as a servant to a ragman, and Carmen brought him one day to the shantytown. He was so impressed that he asked me if he could stay and live with me.

On Sundays we would pray Lauds accompanied by the guitar. All the gypsies would come. I would open up the Scripture and preach the gospel. We would eat together. That poor guy with polio who begged for alms in the metro saw this environment and asked me, "Please, Kiko, let me stay here with you." And he also ended up living with me. But most of all, that whole business with the guys who arrived running away from the police because of drugs produced a terrible conflict in me, because they wouldn't let me sleep. One of them would always come drunk and drugged up, and I had to listen to him for hours and hours. I couldn't say to him, "Let me sleep", because he would become violent—so violent that one day I thought one of these men was going to kill me. That created a terrible fear in me, the fear of death. I wouldn't wish the fear of death on anyone: to live with someone who you think will kill you. It was an unforgettable experience.

I only say this to show that I hardly slept at all, and I would always arrive late to school because I had to take three means of transportation: from the shantytown I had to walk to the bus stop; then, from the bus to the metro at Vallecas and from the metro to the station of Atocha to take another bus that would bring me to the other end of Madrid.

After that scene that the principal made in front of my students, I promised him I would never again arrive late. I told the *quinqui* who would always come to speak to me, "Tomorrow wake me up at five; please. I cannot arrive late." The next day he wakes me up, I wash as best I can and leave. When I went to get the bus, I look behind me and see that the dogs are following me. The people at the bus stop said, "How many dogs! But where are all these animals coming from?"

I pretended there was nothing wrong, looking the other direction. But I was nervous because everyone around was complaining because of those stray dogs. The bus arrived and I got on it quickly. "Phew! Thank goodness!" I thought to myself. But, when I looked behind me, I saw to my horror that the whole pack of dogs was running after the bus!

That had never happened to me. They had never followed the bus before. There were around fifteen dogs. That morning they all came running after me and I thought, "My God, I'm finished!" The bus was full of workers, people going to work. I went to the front of the bus in order to get off as soon as the doors would open and run to the metro. I ran to it, got my ticket and ran down at full speed to the platform. "Phew! Thank goodness!" When I looked behind me, I saw that all the dogs were running down the stairs of the metro. The alarm rang and they called the police.

"And these dogs? You cannot enter the subway with animals! Take them out!" they told me.

"But they aren't mine!"

"What do you mean they aren't yours?"

They brought me to the police. Definitely, I would be late again. The dogs made me arrive late! I think they helped me to be humiliated. When I arrived at the school, I was full of misery and terribly humiliated. Who knows what face the principal saw because he didn't say a word. And why did the dogs follow me specifically that time? It's a mystery! They had never followed me to the bus, and it was even less likely that they would have followed me inside the metro. This is true, it all happened just as I'm telling it.

~

THE TRIPOD IS BORN:
WORD, LITURGY, COMMUNITY

Archbishop Morcillo, the Archbishop of Madrid, with Carmen,
while he greets a quinqui.

In that environment, even with drug addicts and with gypsies, God wanted me to meet Carmen, a missionary who was getting ready to go to India and who also had had contact with Archbishop Manrique to go to Oruro, Bolivia, to work among the miners. She was trying to form a group of evangelizers. We met through her sister, whom I knew because she was part of the group with whom we tried to help the prostitutes and the drug addicts before I went to live with the poor. Carmen had come to the shantytown. Later, she met the group that would meet in my shack. It left a deep impression on her and after that she built herself a shack next to the Bunsen factory, not very far from where I was, and she and one of her friends lived there. God wanted Carmen and me to be together through this work. Carmen is very important for the Way. Through Fr. Farnés, a great liturgist whom she had met in Barcelona, I was put in contact with the renewal of the Second Vatican Council. She always told me the truth, bringing to the Way the full discovery of the Paschal Mystery as it was made mainstream by the Council.

In the shantytown there was such a presence of Jesus Christ, of the Holy Spirit, that some people converted when they went there. Truly, the presence of Jesus Christ was huge in those poor people who welcomed the Word without any pretentions.

Also those guys from prison prayed with an enormous sincerity. I never told them that they didn't have to steal—never, because I felt unworthy. One of those guys had seen his father killed and had been raped three times. They were people "crushed against the wall". And who was I, born in a rich family, a bourgeois, to say anything to him? Why had that boy been abused? Why had he seen his father murdered? What a mystery life is, what a mystery human suffering is! We cannot remain indifferent before it.

We were having a celebration of the Word with the gypsies once a week, and those poor, one way or another, forced me to speak of Christ. And little by little the Christian community began to appear, a community of poor people, because they were gypsies, a woman who had prostituted herself, an old vagabond who would collect cardboard and who lived like human waste; we called him Don Juan. Sometimes we would celebrate the Eucharist. Among the poor, something was beginning to be created. What we now call the "tripod" in the Way was born: the Word, the Eucharist, and the Christian community.

Then the archbishop of Madrid, Archbishop Casimiro Morcillo, came. When I was in the *Cursillos*, one time the archbishop had celebrated a

Mass for all the *cursillistas* in the stadium. Since I was a *Cursillos* instructor, they had introduced me to the archbishop. (This was before I lived in the shantytown). One day the police arrived at the shacks and said that we had to take everything down. The families and all those people were going to be left without a thing. The military police came with submachine guns and two trucks full of workers to take down the shacks. I called some priest friends to come and put themselves there to make some kind of a nonviolent protest.

When the police arrived, I saw that we were lost, that they were going to pull everything down and leave us on the streets. So then the thought occurred to me to call the archbishop. His secretary answered, "Ah, right now he cannot come to the phone!" and he yelled at me.

Providentially, the archbishop, who was a government adviser and a friend of Franco, who wielded a lot of power, asked the secretary, "What's going on?" and the secretary answered, "Nothing, there's someone who's just shouting."

"Who is it?" and he took the phone.

I said, "Father, you have to come here to save these poor people. The only one who can save them is you; otherwise, the police will leave all the people on the streets. There are sick children with measles whose situation can get very serious if they catch cold. And it seems that the police don't care at all!"

The archbishop asked, "Where is this happening?"

And the miracle is that the Archbishop of Madrid showed up in the shantytown! When I told the commander of the military police—who had shown up with a lot of jeeps, because he was afraid of all those gypsies in the shacks—that the Archbishop of Madrid was coming, he could not believe his ears: "What?"

"I'm telling you in all seriousness: the Archbishop is coming!"

He looked at me thinking "And who is this guy to bring an archbishop here?" It was a little bit as though the Pope himself had come! And as a matter of fact, they stopped everything, the police went back to their jeeps and they stayed still on the hill, with the trucks full of workers who were supposed to dismantle the shantytown. They had already taken down Carmen's shack.

Archbishop Casimiro Morcillo arrived in a black car with his secretary. When the commander of the military police saw him, they all left. The Archbishop came inside my shack and was very moved by seeing where I lived. I asked him, "Father, can we sing some psalms?" and the gypsies began to sing. He had such an experience of conversion that he told me, "Kiko, I am not a Christian. Look, from this day onward, my episcopal palace is always open for you." And every time I would go he would give me one thousand pesetas, even though I would say to him, "Father, I don't want anything!" He always supported us in everything.

I asked him, "Father, can we celebrate the Eucharist?" because we had been celebrating the Eucharist in the shack, and that was forbidden at the time, and somebody had denounced us. We had done this because when we went to Mass in the nearby parish, which was in a prefabricated bunker, the dogs and some gypsies came with me, and we were all very dirty, because there was no running water in the shacks. They were full of rats and filth. The people of the parish, when a gypsy of our group would sit next to them, would change seats because he smelled so bad.

The gypsies would say, "Kiko, but those things which you are saying, is it the same as what the priest says?"

"Yes, of course, I'm from that church."

"And those people are Christian? How can they be Christian if they avoid me as if I had the plague?"

I said to the archbishop, "Father, we have understood that neither the people of the parish are ready to welcome these poor people, nor are these people ready to go to the parish."

We were making, let's say, without even wanting to, a ground breaking pastoral work. Like someone who starts making an apostolate in the prisons, we were in an extreme situation. That is why I asked the archbishop, "Father, can we celebrate the Eucharist?"

And he answered me, "Yes, but not in the shack. However, I will make sure that they let you celebrate the Eucharist in the parish." He called the pastor and said, "You have to open the parish for this community of poor people. I allow them to celebrate behind closed doors with home-baked unleavened bread and to receive under both species" (just as we had asked him). I'm speaking of 1965–1966. The Council had just ended and the archbishop told us that we should celebrate behind closed doors, because if someone were to wander in and see the home-baked unleavened bread he could be scandalized. And it was fantastic! In that parish we would sit all around the altar. One day a pastor of a wealthy parish from the neighborhood of Argüelles, a priest who knew me from the time of the *Cursillos*, came. When he saw the Eucharist he was so impressed that he invited us to go to his parish. Carmen, I, and all the gypsies went, and it caused a general shock.

~

A SEED THAT SPREADS

John Paul II with Dino Torreggiani, founder of the Institute of the Servants of the Church, who brought Kiko and Carmen to Rome.

Then, the Lord brought us to a rural environment of peasants. That is to say, the Lord was bringing this little seed that was born among the poor of Palomeras to different social levels, and it began to extend itself. When we were in Avila, a monsignor of Rome, Don Dino Torreggiani, founder of the Servants of the Church—whose process of beatification I've been told is well on its way—heard me preach and told me, "You have to come to Rome. You have to come to Florence, where Don Mazzi is; he is a rebellious priest who, disobeying the cardinal celebrates Mass in the piazza. You have to come to remedy this situation."

"Me? I don't know Italian, I don't know anything!"

We didn't have a penny, we had nothing. But Monsignor Torreggiani managed it. He asked Catholic Action for help, and they paid for our trip to Rome. It was during the time of hippies and long hair. I said to Don Dino, "You don't think I'm going to preach to the long-haired hippies in Piazza Navona or something like that. I want to open a Christian initiation in the parishes."

"OK, then let's go to the parishes." And he accompanied us from parish to parish. He would translate for me. A pastor with whom we were talking said, "Oh, yes, that's all very nice everything you're saying about Christian initiation and baptism and making small communities! Very nice, but just for Spain! We don't need it here. Here we have Catholic Action and everything is going very well. Go back to Spain!"

We went to another one, "Fantastic for Spain. Here we don't need anything." So I said to Don Dino, "Look, Father, I have understood that it is impossible here. You know what? I'm going to go live with the poor in Rome to wait for what God wants from me. Where are the shantytowns here in Rome?"

"In the Borghetto Latino."

There was the parish of St. Jude Thaddeus. I spoke to the pastor and I asked him if there was somewhere for me to stay. He said, "Yes, there is a nun who works in the shantytown." He called her and said, "This man is looking for a place to stay with the poor, in prayer, in contemplation, following the footprints of Charles de Foucauld." So the nun found us a place to stay. A family let us live in the henhouse.

We went to look in the garbage for some junk with which to build a shack. We found some old doors. One man gave me a stove, another a bunk bed, because some seminarians from Avila were with me. Carmen went to live with the nuns of

St. Bridget, in Piazza Navona. I was in the Borghetto Latino, waiting for God to manifest himself. While I was there, one day some young people from the parish of the Canadian Martyrs—I don't know who had told them about me—came by and they left awestruck. They invited me to Lake Nemi, where there was a meeting with all the youth of the base communities, all leftists—these were the times of Che Guevara. I said to them, "You invite me to give my experience?" I used to wear a sort of green jacket, like Fidel Castro and I had a long beard. "Careful because you run a great risk." And there, in an assembly, all leftist young people, I said that Lenin and Che Guevara were false prophets, and I spoke of Christ, who doesn't resist evil, throwing to the ground all their ideas. They were stunned. But a little group that was there and that played guitars at a Mass in the parish of the Canadian Martyrs (they called it the "beat Mass" and it was full of young people) invited me to see that Mass. I saw it. They asked me, "What do you think?"

I answered, "You don't renew the Church with guitars."

"No? Then how?"

"With the Paschal Mystery, with the Kerygma."

"And what is that?" they had never heard of the Kerygma.

"Well, if you want, I can explain it to you."

I spoke to the group that would lead those young people, and I prepared with them a sort of convivence (retreat) on a mountain with a priest. And I preached the Kerygma to them, the Paschal mystery, and the Christian initiation, and they were left very surprised. They told me, "Why don't we begin this in the parish?" I said to them, "No. We cannot begin only with young people, because the Church is not only for them, it is for everyone. If you invite some married couples, I'll give the catechesis." And they did just that, and we formed the first community in the parish of the Canadian Martyrs.

Then I went to Florence. Another battle! We began in a very poor parish, in a garage. Then they invited us to go to Portugal and we went there also to live with the poor, in a neighborhood of shacks in Lisbon called "A Corraleira". One year later we went back to visit the community of Rome. They had obeyed everything we had said to them, the tripod: to celebrate the Word of God one day of the week, to celebrate the Eucharist, and once a month for everyone to give their experience of how God was acting in their own history.

After that, three other parishes in Rome wanted the Way: the parish of the Nativity, where the pastor was Don Luigi Della Torre, who was a famous liturgist (he had met us and was very impressed); the parish of San Aloysius Gonzaga in the neighborhood of the Parioli, an upper-class neighborhood of Rome; and the parish of St. Frances Cabrini, very near the Canadian Martyrs parish. These are the only four parishes that we personally have opened in Rome. Later, when they began to ask for more catecheses, catechists from these parishes helped, and today in Rome the Way exists in maybe one hundred parishes, and there are some five hundred communities.

The Way is in almost all the dioceses of Spain and Italy and has spread to more than 120 nations, with thousands of communities. God is doing a work that is surprising to us, despite our sins.

I have told a little bit of my experience and I find myself today surprised at the many wonders the Lord is accomplishing and has already accomplished with us. It is as if I am condemned to tell this story showing myself as living proof, accepting also to be judged like someone who thinks he is a saint, a vain man, a presumptuous man, or something of that sort. The truth is that everything surpasses us, and when I look back, all the things that the Lord has done with me seem incredible.

~

Some Historical Photographs of the Shantytown

The inside of Kiko's shack.

The outside of Kiko's shack.

The inside of Kiko's shack: his bedroom and the mattress that he used to sleep on on the floor.

Kiko with the first brothers who went to live with him, Manolo (left), and Domingo; behind, the wall of the shack with an image of St. Francis of Assisi.

Kiko at the door of his shack in the Borghetto Latino of Rome.

The Abbè Pierre, founder of the Emmaus Movement. In the photograph, at the left, Mariano and Joaquín with their families, and to the right, Kiko and Jorge.

To the left Manolo and to the right Joaquin, with his two daughters and his wife on the donkey, and Kiko.

The Archbishop of Madrid, Archbishop Morcillo, the pastor of the parish of the Colonia Sandi, and José Agudo (head of a group of gypsies), singing a psalm in Kiko's shack.

José Agudo and his wife Rosario.

*Carmen Hernández
in Jerusalem.*

*Archbishop Morcillo asked the
pastor of la Colonia Sandi to
allow this wooden structure,
where some parish activities
were held, to be used by the
community of the shantytown.*

*A priest and Carmen with all
the things that they managed to
salvage from Carmen's shack
shortly after the police knocked
it down.*

Kiko, Carmen, and Fr. Mario.

THE KERYGMA

THEOLOGICAL COMMENTARY

Christoph Cardinal Schönborn

In a few days the Year of Faith will begin and also the Synod on the New Evangelization. It is a favorable moment for publishing the catechesis that Kiko Argüello delivered in Sora during June of this year [2012].

This catechesis of the "Three Angels" is a strong and powerful Word for the Year of Faith. " 'Faith comes from what is heard' [Rom 10:17]. 'But how are men to call upon him in whom they have not believed? And how are they to believe in him of whom they have never heard? And how are they to hear without a preacher? And how can men preach unless they are sent? As it is written, 'How beautiful are the feet of those who preach good news!' " (Rom 10:14–15).

The Neocatechumenal Way is an itinerary of "Christian initiation" and of "permanent education in faith" that has been recognized many times by the Church as a "gift of the Holy Spirit". But above all, it is a way of evangelization for our times. This way—confirmed and encouraged time and again by the popes Paul VI, Blessed John Paul II, and Benedict XVI—has opened the door to faith for many people through the announcement of the good news, the *Kerygma*. The new life of Christ has entered into the lives of many people through this door of faith. The grace of faith has brought about conversions; healing; a Yes to life, to children; to being able to forgive and the willingness to be sent on a mission.

All over the world, communities have been formed that have truly become bearers of the evangelization to the ends of the earth. The gospel has been taken to the most remote parts of the world thanks to families in mission and the *missio ad gentes*. It is truly astonishing to see how hundreds of large families stand up and make themselves available for the mission, for the New Evangelization: "Here we are, Lord! Send us!"

These numerous missionaries of our times are able to offer their disposition to go on mission because they have first lived an intense way of Christian catechesis. To transform people into disciples of Christ, to win them for Christ, we must first have personally attended Jesus' "school of life"— we must have developed an intimacy with him, have allowed him to instruct, form, and shape us, time and again—so that he can truly send out his disciples.

Kiko's catechesis, published here, is a strong "lesson for disciples". It is a call to personal conversion. What touched me in this catechesis is that it shows clearly (and personally to me) that you cannot evangelize without personal conversion. The missionary himself must first be evangelized. And this conversion is never settled once and for all. I cannot say "I've already been evangelized!" Of course I can say: "I believe in God! I love him! I want to give him my entire life!" Nevertheless, I am still aware that sin continues to act within me and that I need salvation every day: "Apart from me you can do nothing" (Jn 15:5).

This catechesis is a strong and beautiful example of the "evangelization of the evangelists". Those who would become "angels"—that is, messengers of the good news—must first meet the work of the first and second angel: the work of the seducer, the "liar from the beginning", the "prince of this world" and also the work of the angel of the Gospel who brought the announcement to Mary.

In this catechesis the entire announcement of the gospel is impressively condensed.

May this catechesis be heard by many; may it touch the hearts of many, so that through it they can be strengthened in faith and inflamed with love. Because the New Evangelization can only reach the hearts of men if "the love of Christ urges us on" (2 Cor 5:14).

CHRISTOPH CARDINAL SCHÖNBORN
Archbishop of Vienna
October 2, 2012
Feast of the Guardian Angels

KERYGMA

"The Three Angels"

Abbey of St. Dominic in Sora
June 8, 2012

I would like to begin with a song to the Virgin Mary, who has inspired the Neocatechumenal Way. As you know, Pope Benedict XVI, in the audience he granted us last January 20, [2012], affirmed once again that the Way is "a gift of the Holy Spirit to help the Church". The Neocatechumenal Way opens an itinerary of Christian initiation and of permanent education in the faith in the parishes, that is, a concrete way of forming adult Christians. It is a Way primarily for those far from the Church. Thanks to the long and serious process of formation in the faith that is the Way, we offer to a pagan, to a person far from the Church, to a secularized man the possibility of becoming a new man, a new creation, a child of God, capable of living in Christ and for Christ and not alone, but in a Christian community that announces to the world the truth of the love of God.

You have chosen as a motto of this meeting "A Millennium of the Abbey of Sora and the New Evangelization". Well, as you know, when we begin the Way in a parish, we tell the pastor that it is necessary and urgent to pass from a pastoral of sacramentalization to a pastoral of evangelization, understanding pastoral of evangelization as bringing the gospel to so many who do not know it or have abandoned the Church.

In your towns and cities, as well as everywhere else today, there is degradation among the youth;

married couples separate, they divorce. . . . The Neocatechumenal Way, thanks be to God, is rebuilding so many families. These rebuilt families, open to life, are full of children, of young people, to whom they transmit faith. We find this joy: we have thousands and thousands of youth in the communities.

Remember, for example, that the Way brought about 300,000 young people to the last World Youth Day in Madrid. There we had a fantastic vocational meeting, presided by Cardinal Rouco, archbishop of Madrid, and with the participation of thirteen other cardinals and about a hundred bishops. As you know, the Lord is preparing the Neocatechumenal Way for a new evangelization in the entire world, but especially in Asia. The Lord has inspired us with the task of preparing 20,000 priests for China. In that meeting I invited the youth to offer themselves to God for this task of re-evangelizing China, where there are 1,300 million people who do not know Christ. As you know, about 5,000 young men stood up and came to the stage. We did not know where to put them. The stage was huge, but not big enough, so we decided to have them come up in two shifts to receive the blessing from the bishops. And afterward 3,000 young women stood up. (I was happy because they told me that they were thinking of taking up a collection at the end of this meeting for the evangelization of China. I thought that was an excellent initiative.)

I was saying that it is necessary to pass from a pastoral of sacramentalization to a pastoral of evangelization in the parish. Because if the parish has, let us suppose, about fifteen thousand people living in its geographical boundaries, only five or ten percent of these continue to come to Mass on Sundays; there is still a group of people who get married in the church, who baptize their children, and so on. But there is another huge number of people that no longer go to church. How do we reach so many secularized people? There is an enormous crisis, in this sense, throughout Europe. Consider that in France, for example, fifty percent of people are no longer baptized. In Spain there is also a high percentage. John Paul II spoke about the apostasy of Europe.

We tell the pastor that the pastoral ministry of sacramentalization nurtures the people who still have faith. Christ is present in the sacraments: in baptism, in the Eucharist, and so forth. We say that the sacramental pastoral ministry is good for those people who have that faith and still come to the Church to meet Christ present in the sacraments. But, how can we reach all the others, those who do not have faith? We need a presence of Christ that does not require faith, a presence of Christ that attracts all men, even those who no longer have faith. Does that presence exist?

In the Way we say that that presence is to be found in the gospel. Christ says: "Love one another; even as I have loved you. . . . By this all men will know that you are my disciples" (Jn 13:34–35). Pay attention to "as I have loved you", because it is fundamental. A special love is needed. I do not know if you have ever seen this kind of love made present, made flesh, made a sacrament, a sign. "Love as I have loved you." Christ has loved us when we were his enemies, when we were sinners, evil. It is love to the enemy. Have you ever seen a Christian who loves his enemy? Where is that love? Where can this love be seen? Because Christ says: "Love one another; even as I have loved you. . . . By this all men will know that you are my disciples." In other words: "Love one another as I have loved you"—that is, in this dimension of love to the enemy—"by this all men will know that you are my disciples." That is, in this love, all, even people who are secularized, those who are far away or out of the Church, will say: look, those are disciples of Christ!

But there is more. Jesus Christ also says: "Father . . . I in them and you in me, that they may become perfectly one"—pay attention to the word "perfectly one"—"so that the world may know that you have sent me" (Jn 17:23). That is, if we are perfectly one, the world will believe, the pagans will believe.

In order for faith to arise in the far away, they will have to see these signs of faith: love to the enemy and perfect unity. This is what the Way wants to do: to form Christian communities that will give these two signs; love for the enemy, love in the dimension of the cross, and perfect unity, that relationship of the Divine Persons that is found in the Holy Trinity. These signs of love and unity are the light of the world!

To Open Our Ears

How do we get to the point that a Christian community reaches this stature of faith? Through a Christian initiation, through a long and serious process. Thank God today we have communities that have finished the Neocatechumenal itinerary and many families in these communities are leaving for the *missio ad gentes* throughout Europe and the entire world. We now also have the *communitates in missionem*. In Rome the Pope has sent the first fifteen communities in mission. If in a parish we have, for example, thirty communities, five of them are sent to help parishes in the suburbs of Rome that are full of immigrants (Chinese and Romanians, for example) and they need help.

I am giving only a rough sketch, some brush-strokes, making some brief allusions so that you may understand the great mission to which God is calling us.

"Faith comes from what is heard" (Rom 10:17). "It pleased God through the folly of what we preach to save those who believe" (1 Cor 1:21). St. Paul, who writes in Greek, says that God wanted to save the world through the foolishness of the Kerygma, which is what, God willing, I am about to announce to you.

But there is a problem in the world: people who have left the Church do not listen; their ears are closed. You can go through the streets announcing all the Kerygmas you want, but the people have their ears closed and say, "Bah! All that is nonsense!" That is why opening people's ears to get them ready to listen is the most urgent thing. And how can the ears of the pagan, secularized, atheist or agnostic world be opened? How?

In the Acts of the Apostles they say how: through miracles. In the Acts each Kerygma is preceded by a miracle that creates amazement, that creates surprise, that opens the ears of the people to prepare them to listen. Because faith comes through the ears.

The first miracle that appears in the Acts of the Apostles takes place on the day of Pentecost:

the miracle of tongues. People of different nations (Parthians, Medes, Elamites, Arabs, for example) heard St. Peter in their own languages as he announced the Kerygma: "Jesus of Nazareth . . . you crucified and killed by the hands of lawless men. But God raised him up, having loosed the pangs of death . . . God has made him both Lord *Kyrios* and Christ, this Jesus whom you crucified" (Acts 2:22–24, 36). In the Old Testament the word *Kyrios* refers to God. This Jesus is the Lord, is God. Later on there is the miracle of the cure of the paralytic in the Temple entrance called "the Beautiful Gate", and others. These are miracles that prepare the people to listen to the announcement of the good news, the great news that saves the world.

However, curiously, these miracles stop at a certain point, since a physical miracle is somehow limited: it reaches only those who are present there, at that moment, those who have witnessed it. Why does it seem that in Acts the physical miracles stop? Because the real miracle appears, what theology calls the "moral miracle": the Church. When the Christian community appears, love and unity made flesh appear. The Holy Spirit descends upon the people and makes of them a new creation. A new relationship appears: Love. "See how they love each other", said the pagans seeing the Christians. This, little by little, saves the world.

In one of the *missio ad gentes* that we opened, a short time ago a Ukrainian girl, an atheist who was raised under communism, has asked to be baptized. When they inquired as to why, she answered, "Because I am astonished at the way you relate to one another. I am a babysitter for one of the families in the community. Others come to their house to prepare the celebration; I am surprised at the way you relate to one another." That is, she realizes that the relationship we Christians have is not merely human, that we are not simple friends who play cards or belong to the same club, and so on. What unites us? The Holy Spirit. This relationship in the Holy Spirit is a sign for the world. "Love one another." The love is given in the Holy Spirit. "God is love" (1 Jn 4:8). This girl asks for baptism because she would like to love as we love one another. She says, "I am alone and I feel lonely. I would like really to love someone, but I do not love anyone. I am always angry at myself and at everyone else."

These are the signs that call to faith: love and unity. Europe is secularized; it is losing faith. The people do not believe in the temples; they do not believe in priests or in religious signs. But when they see the love among us they ask for baptism. This is how we have created communities among the pagans in Amsterdam, in Almere, in Chemnitz, for example. We are forming communities faster among the pagans than among the people of the parishes.

But, for this, there have to be families available. Last Sunday we had a meeting in Milan, on the occasion of the World Family Day with the Pope. I asked for missionaries for the New Evangelization and almost two thousand families stood up. A river of people, because married couples came up with all their children. A never-ending river! There are brothers and sisters in the communities that offer themselves to go to any part of the world with all their children to evangelize. They are the fruits of years and years of work in towns, in cities, in the suburbs.

THE ANNOUNCEMENT OF SALVATION

Well, brothers and sisters, this has been a kind of admonition. Now, before listening to a reading from the Holy Scriptures and saying something to you, briefly announcing the Kerygma, I want to sing, as I always do, a song to the Virgin Mary. I also want to ask your prayers, because tomorrow we will go to Budapest, where they have asked us to have a meeting in the most important square in the city, with the brothers and sisters of Hungary and the parishioners of the parishes of Budapest. In Hungary we have two *missio ad gentes*, in completely secularized areas, where almost no one comes to Mass. Recall that Hungary has been under Communism, under atheism for many years.

Song: "Mary House of All Blessing"

Mary House of All Blessing
Salvation for our age,
Earthly abode of the humble one
You as in Cana of Galilee
You had seen that we were lacking wine;
That our feast was not a feast
That our life was not life
Because death was reigning over us.
You have brought us to your Son
You have taught us to obey him
And to do whatever he tells us
So that he would turn our water
Into new wine
Victory! Victory! Eternal life in Christ Risen!
Alleluia! Allelu! Alleluia!
Alleluia! Allelu! Alleluia!

Well, now I will attempt, in spite of my tiredness and difficulties, to make the announcement of the Kerygma. Recently we had a meeting in Trieste and it was fantastic. Afterward we had one in the United States (in Chicago, where hundreds of families, young men and women stood up for the mission in China). Then we had a meeting in Naples presided by Cardinal Sepe, archbishop of Naples, in the Piazza del Plebiscito, which was full of brothers and sisters, more than forty thousand. The Lord Jesus went from town to town announcing the Kingdom. That is why I am moved by the fact that the Lord has brought us here and I am happy to be able to announce Jesus Christ.

There is nothing greater in the world than the announcement of the gospel. "God wanted to save the world through the foolishness of the Kerygma." The Kerygma is not a sermon, it is not a reflection. What is the Kerygma? It is the announcement of a news that is realized every time that it is proclaimed. And what does it realize? Salvation. If today I announce the Kerygma to you, again salvation takes place among you. "God has wanted to save the world through the foolishness of the kerygma." This news that is made present, makes present a fact, something that becomes real, something that becomes a reality. That is why the announcement of the gospel is so important. The word "gospel" means good news, good message, "gospel" and "Kerygma" are the same. To announce the gospel is to announce the Kerygma. It is important to be able to listen to the Kerygma.

It is very important to announce it, and the Lord has not allowed me to marry, so that I can dedicate myself completely to this mission, so that you may be able to listen to it. "Follow me", the Lord Jesus said to someone. He answered: "Let me first go and bury my father." Jesus told him: "Let the dead bury their own dead; but as for you, go and proclaim the Kingdom of God" (Lk 9:59–60). Through something that looks like foolishness, by talking of and giving the news, the eternal salvation of men comes, makes itself present.

Normally, before announcing the Kerygma, I proclaim a Word from the New Testament. I always carry the Scripture with me. I have been carrying the Bible with me, always, for forty-five years. I was impressed, the other day, with a reading in which St. Jerome tells the priests, "Always have the Sacred Scriptures with you, the Holy Scripture, the Bible."

Many times I proclaim a Word that you know very well, which you have heard often in the announcement of the Kerygma, a Word that is very important to me, because it says: "Behold, *now* is the acceptable time; behold, *now* is the day of salvation" (2 Cor 6:2, italics added). This "now" is very interesting, it is perfect, because it means that when the gospel is announced, in that precise moment, salvation takes place. We find an echo of this in the Sermon on the Mount, when the Lord says: "Blessed are you that hunger *now*, for you shall be satisfied. . . . Woe to you that are full *now*, for you shall hunger" (Lk 6:21, 25, italics added). It speaks of a precise moment: of the "now".

Even though you have heard me speak other times, I will not say things that you already have heard, because the preaching is always new, because it is a work done by the Holy Spirit, who accompanies those who announce the gospel. And the most important thing that the Holy Spirit does is not so much to inspire those who preach—he also does this, which is undoubtedly very important—but rather to enter the one who is listening, so that he may believe the announcement. We need the Holy Spirit both to say what I am about to say and for you to believe what I will announce. As St. Paul said: "No one can say 'Jesus is Lord' except by the Holy Spirit" (1 Cor 12:3). In order to believe what I say, we need the Holy Spirit, who is in you and testifies it to you, seals it in you. It is not a rational thing. It is not that you adhere to a rational truth or anything like that. No. In order for you to believe what I am saying, you need that the Holy Spirit witnesses it inside you.

And this always takes place while respecting your free will. Always. That is why it is a mystery when someone listens and welcomes the announcement of the Kerygma. One will be taken and the other left (see Lk 17:34). One listens and his life changes, thanks to the fact that the Word penetrates into him. This is faith according to St. Paul. St. Paul says (see Rom 8:16) that the Spirit of Christ descends from heaven and entering into man, it gives witness to the spirit of that man that God exists, that God loves him, that God is his Father, that God loves him as a son. This internal witness of the Holy Spirit is, as St. John of the Cross says, a "touch of substance". This witness opens your eyes, transforms you. It is the work of the Holy Spirit that accompanies the evangelizers.

That is why, what I say is not as important as the fact that God has chosen you, that he has foreseen that today, here in Sora, at this hour of the night, he will give you a "Word of Salvation" (see Acts 13:26) that can change your life. We have so many testimonies from people whose lives were almost destroyed, witnessing that in a meeting a Word has transformed their lives.

That is why, I tell you right now, to you who today will receive a Word of Salvation, a gift that will strengthen your faith, that will make you grow in faith, that will help you in your way toward heaven: *Congratulations!* That is why I am here to do this priceless service: Salvation! That is why I do it for free: it is truly beyond any price.

It was God who has brought me here. Why? Perhaps because one of you here is in mortal sin? Because perhaps he is having an affair with a woman? Because he has I do not know what problem? God is capable of moving the whole world for one person. God has pulled the strings to have me come here.

Our Lord is full of love, of mercy, of tenderness. Above all he is full of love for the sinners, of love for us sinners, for the thieves, the adulterous, the false, those who always lie, those who rob, those who gamble. God has a great love, great, immense, for each man, to the point of giving his life for the most treacherous man, for the child abuser, for the worst scum. God has given his life for him.

Listen to this Word of St. Paul to the Corinthians:

For the love of Christ urges us on, because we are convinced that one has died for all; therefore all have died. And he died for all, that those who live might live no longer for themselves but for him who for their sake died and was raised.

[102]

From now on, therefore, we regard no one according to the flesh; even though we once regarded Christ according to the flesh, we regard him thus no longer. Therefore, if any one is in Christ, he is a new creation; the old has passed away, behold, the new has come. All this is from God, who through Christ reconciled us to himself and gave us the ministry of reconciliation; that is, in Christ God was reconciling the world to himself, not counting their trespasses against them and entrusting to us the message of reconciliation. So we are ambassadors for Christ, God making his appeal through us. We beg you on behalf of Christ, be reconciled to God. For our sake he made him to be sin who knew no sin, so that in him we might become the righteousness of God.

Working together with him, then, we entreat you not to accept the grace of God in vain. For he says,

"At the acceptable time I have listened to you and helped you on the day of salvation."

Behold, now is the acceptable time; behold, now is the day of salvation (2 Cor 5:14–21; 6:1–2).

We've just heard it: now is the moment of your salvation. That is why it is extremely important that you all listen well. Let us listen! The Lord wants to tell you good news, good news, a fantastic thing. What does the kerygma say? What is this announcement? What does the kerygma announce? It announces an extremely important fact: God has sent his Son for all of us, to give his life for all of us.

We have heard St. Paul tell us: "The love of Christ urges us on", it is urgent, to think that if one died for all, all men have died. And all men can freely receive eternal life, immortal life, because Christ has given his life for all!

And how can we bring immortal life, eternal life to men? How can we give them this news? That is evangelization. It is not easy. It is not that one goes and speaks and that's it, because, as I said before, the people have their ears closed; they are against the Church; they are scandalized about a priest in school or who knows where. The people are not willing to listen. But St. Paul says: "Christ has died for all." What for? For what has Christ died? St. Paul repeats: "Christ died for all, so that they may not live for themselves."

To live for themselves. What does it mean to live for oneself? All live for themselves. To live for oneself is to live looking for your own happiness. All live looking for their own happiness. A young man, for instance, goes to the university, has a girlfriend, looks for a job, and so on, looking for his own happiness in all things. And what's so bad about this?

It is important that you understand this; I am speaking of one aspect of the Kerygma. The Kerygma is like a prism: it has many facets and each one of its facets shines. This that St. Paul says is a very existential aspect of the Kerygma; it has its origin in what we call original sin. The sin of the origin.

Original sin, Scripture tells us, is the sin that our first parents, Adam and Eve, committed. God created men, Adam and Eve, in a paradise. He gave them the gifts called *preternatural gifts*—immortality, for example. God did not create death. Scripture says: "God created man for incorruption . . . but through the devil's envy death entered the world" (Wis 2:23–24). Another gift: harmony with all animals. Many wonderful gifts. And the greatest gift: friendship with God, a loving relationship with him.

Scripture speaks of a dialogue between the woman and an angel (see Gen 3). Imagine that here on the left there is a woman and an angel; here in the center there is another woman and another angel; and here on the right a third woman and a third angel.

THE FIRST ANGEL AND THE FIRST DIALOGUE: THE WOMAN AND THE SERPENT

The first angel dialogues with the woman; the woman listens and through this dialogue sin enters into the world. It is interesting to know what this first angel says. His name is Lucifer, beautiful light, the most handsome angel in heaven, but he rebels against God, because he does not accept his condition of creature and wants to take the place of God. This angel presents himself to the first woman, Eve, under the aspect of an animal, in the form of a serpent, to establish a dialogue with her. He tells the first lie, "Did God say, 'You shall not eat of any tree of the garden.'?" And the woman replies to the angel that it is not true. "We may eat of the trees of the garden." She explains that this is the only tree of which they cannot eat—they were next to a special tree—the tree of the knowledge of good and evil, because God told them not to eat of it, because if they did they will die. And the angel continues, speaking to Eve, "No way! It is not true that you will die!" The second lie! Look what Jesus tells the Pharisees, "Why do you not understand what I say? It is because you cannot bear to hear my word. You are of your father the devil. . . . He was a murderer from the beginning. . . . When he lies, he speaks according to his own nature, for he is a liar and the father of lies" (Jn 8:43–44). Christ says this when he speaks of the devil in Chapter 8 of St. John.

The angel tells Eve, "You will not die. For God knows that when you eat of it your eyes will be open and you will be like God, knowing good and evil." In effect he was saying, "Now you know the good, the Love of God. When you experience doing evil, eating—not by hearsay but actually having the experience—you will know, like God, good and evil. Then you will not need anyone to explain anything to you. You will decide between good and evil. You will be like God."

And Genesis says that Eve looking at the beauty of becoming like God ate. That is, she has heard that kind of catechesis from this angel and has to answer this dialogue and answers by saying "Amen" to the lies the devil is telling her. St. Paul says that the devil, finding opportunity in the law, of the Torah, seduced us and killed us (see Rom 7:11). This tree, in effect, is an image of the Torah, of the divine law, of the Ten Commandments, because it is God who says what is good and evil. God has pronounced the Ten Words: "You shall not commit adultery and he who does so will die.

You shall not lie. You shall not steal. You shall not covet your neighbor's wife. . . ." But the devil has said that all these prohibitions, which God established, are there to "castrate" you. "Because God is jealous of you and does not want you to realize yourself as God, as he is."

By eating of the fruit, Eve and Adam allow sin to enter them. And this sin inhabits the flesh of man. But—pay attention now because this is extremely important!—What is the result of that sin? The result is death. But not only physical or natural death. We insist on something else; as the philosopher Kierkegaard also said: the worst effect of sin is "ontological death" the death in the most profound part of our being, the death of what makes us be persons.

The word "person" as well as the word "personage" come from the Greek word *prosopon*, which were the masks that actors wore in the theater to represent their personage. The director of the play in the theater assigns to each actor a role, a character: "You will be the prince. You will be a soldier", and so forth. That is, a mission has been given to each one of us in this life, a role in the play, let us say. Thus, we are persons if we exist for someone else, if someone else gives us a role, a being. But if the devil tells you that there is no director, that there is no God, because God is a jealous one, a monster, then God does not exist and you are god of yourself. At that moment the most profound roots of your being as person have died. Who has created you? Who knows! What do you live for? I don't know! What is your role in the world, in this "theatrical work"? I don't know!

Because of sin you have lost the most profound dimension of yourself, what makes you be a person. Indeed, man, by separating himself from God, who is the only one who is—"I AM WHO I AM" (Ex 3:14)—finds out that he *is not*.

But man wants to be, to be also in the others: to be in the love of a woman, in the love of the parents, of a girl, to be for someone else. Do you know the number of young people who commit suicide? One of the fundamental reasons that so many young people kill themselves in the world —in Europe there are thousands and thousands— is *not being*, to discover that they *are not* for anyone. A young man in Sweden, for example, has lived through his parents' separation: his mother lives with another man; his father with another woman. They meet him once in a while, only to give him money. He studies in the university. He has relations with one girl for a time, then with another. With the last one he thought things were going well until he found out that she went to bed with his best friend. At that moment he thinks about suicide. Why? Because he sees that he *is* for no one, he does not exist, no one loves him.

Another fact. Two young sportsmen were traveling in a ferry from Finland to Sweden. Near them there was a very beautiful girl of about sixteen, looking at the sea. Suddenly both see her climbing the rail and throwing herself overboard into the dark sea. They are stunned. They run to tell the captain, "Stop the ship! A girl has fallen into the sea!" The captain answers, "Stop the ship? Imagine that! Two out of three young people throw themselves into the sea. If we had to stop the ship every time. . . . Calm down, she is already dead. This sea is very cold, and they only survive five minutes." The young men were extremely shocked. This is a true story.

People kill themselves because they *are not* for anyone. To be! Remember the story of that Italian family: a good family, very well educated. The husband killed his two daughters, very cute, blonde, and then he killed himself. They are still looking for the bodies of the girls. The wife says, "I can't believe it. I don't understand. That is not the man I married and with whom I have lived all these years. I married and lived with a friendly guy, good looking, very intelligent, and educated. I don't understand."

We know why. Why do they continue killing women? Why do they continue killing children? Why the other day in Spain did a man kill and burn his children? Certainly he had received First Communion and went to Mass, but since college he had stopped going to church. John Paul II said that if a baptized person stops practicing his faith and decides to be the one who directs his life, it's as if his baptism were dead.

When one puts all his being into the love of a woman who, he thinks, loves him, and that woman falls in love with someone else and leaves him, then man experiences in himself something that he did not know: hell. Immediately he experiences within himself a horror, an abyss is opened before him. He goes from being to not being; he does not exist; he experiences total darkness, an abyss of darkness. This suffering is so great that he asks himself "How can I make my wife understand the harm, the tremendous evil that she had done to me?" And he thinks, "By killing the children!"

To Offer Oneself Everything

Every four minutes a married couple breaks up in Spain and in Italy. Everywhere married couples are separating more and more frequently. And women continue to be killed. Because of your baptism you are prophets, and you know the reason why things happen. We can explain it. But to do so, we have to announce Jesus Christ, and people do not want to hear sermons or religious things.

What I have told you are examples. Sin has entered man's flesh and has left its consequences. Original sin has an infinite dimension. It has closed heaven and has brought man, the whole of humanity, to hell, to be under the dominion of death. Consider that even saints like Abraham, Isaac, Moses, David could not enter heaven. They had to remain in Sheol, because heaven was closed. Why? Because it is not the same to slap a child or to slap a policeman, or the head of state. Right? Well original sin has an infinite weight, an infinite value; because it has offended God and we could only be redeemed by God himself. Christ is God, and that is why his redeeming death has an infinite value and was able to open heaven for all mankind. Are you aware of this? Christ is risen; he has opened heaven, and he has taken with him to paradise first Adam and Eve and then Abraham, Isaac, Moses, David, and all the holy patriarchs who were awaiting salvation. Christ went down into hell; he broke the gates of hell and from there rescued Adam and Eve, our parents of old, and brought them to heaven.

All mankind is under the dominion of death and we must announce the good news. Olivier Clement, an Orthodox theologian who is very close to Catholicism, says that original sin obliges man to offer everything to himself. That is why St. Paul says that Christ has died so that men may no longer live for themselves. Sin that dwells in our flesh obliges us to offer everything to ourselves: all the women for me, everything for me, everything for my happiness. I look for myself in everything; I look for my pleasure in everything, that is why I am a selfish man.

In chapter 7 of the Letter to the Romans (see Rom 7:15–23) St. Paul says: I do not understand what's wrong with me, I know the truth with my intellect and the law of God; that is, I know that to love is the truth; but I experience in my flesh, in my members, another law. That wanting to do that which is good, I end up doing the evil that I don't want to do.

It often happens, for instance, that a man works in an office; he is in love with his wife, he has three children, but he begins to look at a new secretary who has just started working there and who is very cute. He does not like to look at her like that, but he does. He does not like to talk to her in a suggestive way, but he does. He does not want to touch her, but he does touch her. He does not like to betray his wife, but he does. And afterward he regrets it. He doesn't understand what has happened to him. St. Paul says: "I do not do what I want, but I do the very thing I hate. . . . Now if I do what I do not want, it is no longer I that do it, but sin which dwells within me . . . making me captive to the law of sin" (see Rom 7:14–23). Sin that dwells in my flesh enslaves me to the law of the concupiscence of the flesh, because now my being is dead. I want to be happy and use nature, sexuality, for instance, which is a beautiful thing that God has created; I distort it and use it to fill the profound emptiness that I feel.

But man is not satisfied even if he has a marvelous wife. Let me give you an example: a man has divorced twice. His latest wife is fifteen years younger than he is. She is very beautiful. He is a successful businessman. He has two children: one studies in London; the other, in New York. He is in the Canary Islands with his yacht, eating and having a good time with his friends and is apparently very happy. Why did he that very night throw himself out from the seventh floor of the hotel? Tell me: Why? He has a wonderful wife, he has two wonderful children, and he is enjoying his yacht on the sea. Why did he kill himself? Those of you who are priests should be able to explain it to the people. Do you know why? Because it has been many years since he has loved anyone. Life is not only to be successful at work, to go on a yacht. Life is to love, to love! And this man realizes that for a long time he has not loved anyone. Can one live without loving?

Original sin—we are Catholics—has not destroyed man's nature completely. The *Catechism of the Catholic Church* says that original sin has wounded man (CCC 406–7). We are wounded! All of us know in the depth of ourselves that to love, to help those in need, to participate in some activities for the poorest, to help Africa, as so many organizations do, is good and beautiful. But then we find another profound reality: "When I want to do right, evil lies close at hand" (Rom 7:21). That is why St. Paul says: "Wretched man that I am! Who will deliver me from this body of death? Thanks be to God through Jesus Christ our Lord!" (Rom 7:24–25) This is the first dialogue.

THE SECOND ANGEL AND THE SECOND DIALOGUE: THE ANNOUNCEMENT TO THE BLESSED VIRGIN MARY

Here in the center there is another dialogue between another angel and a woman named Mary, a young girl. The angel brings her good news: "Rejoice Mary. You are full of the love of God, full of the grace of the Lord. God has chosen you. From you the Son of God will be born!" Imagine: the angel tells a young girl that she is going to be the Mother of God, the Holy *Theotokos*, as the Eastern Church calls her, the highest title for a woman.

The Virgin has to answer this dialogue and answers saying, "May it be done unto me according to your Word, according to what you have said to me." Then, if in the first dialogue sin immediately enters in the human flesh, in this second dialogue the Holy Spirit immediately descends on the Virgin Mary and begins to gestate in her our Lord Jesus Christ, who comes, thanks to her, to do an immense work, to save mankind.

If sin has as a consequence the most profound death of mankind and hell as its recompense and outcome, Christ comes to save the whole of humanity, offering himself for the sin of men, extirpating sin from the flesh of man. This is his work: to take away sin from man and to open heaven.

A young man could ask me, "Kiko, are you saying that all the sufferings I went through are a consequence of the sin that dwells in me? Are you saying that I carry within me a principle that makes me look out for myself in everything? That I am a selfish man, and because of this I slept with my friend's wife and I have stolen at work? That this is why many times I lie and that it's this that makes me suffer so much? Are you saying that the cause of all my sufferings is a principle that I carry within me and it is called sin? Well, no one has ever told me these things! Are you saying that I could be freed if they took away from me the sin that I carry in my flesh? Well, then, take sin away from me!"

And what do I have to do to take away sin? I take that young man to a parish where there is the Neocatechumenal Way, for instance one of those parishes where we have built a *catechumenium*, a new church with the [icons of the life of Christ as a] *crown of mysteries*, with a baptismal pool, where we baptize the pagans by immersion during the Easter Vigil, and I tell him, "Do you see this pool? If you enter into it, sin will be taken away from you."

"Then put me into it immediately."

"Before receiving baptism, first you have to do a catechumenate."

Baptism takes away original sin, forgives all sins, and makes of us a new creation. This is the work that Jesus Christ comes to do. He offered himself to the Father as propitiation for all men. We can announce to every man that in Christ he can receive the forgiveness of all his sins. And, if all his sins are forgiven him, from heaven he can receive the Holy Spirit, who makes of him a new creation, a child of God. Not all men are children of God. All are divine creatures. But to become a child of God it is necessary to give an answer to grace. And the answer is personal. God does not impose salvation on anyone. That is why Jesus Christ offered himself to the Father on the cross for each man.

Imagine what this means: *"Caritas Christi urget nos!"* "The love of Christ urges us on, because we are convinced that one has died for all; therefore all have died. And he died for all, that those who live might live no longer for themselves but for him who for their sake died and was raised" (2 Cor 5:14–15). Look! What zeal! *"Caritas Christi urget nos"* is an expression of zeal. There is no true Christian who has no zeal, because the zeal to save mankind comes from the Father, not from us. It is the Father who wants all men to be saved (see 1 Tim 2:4). What a mystery! And why doesn't he save them directly? Why doesn't he send them an angel who would appear to them at night? Why doesn't he make them experience a miracle? Well, no: "It pleased God through the folly of what we preach to save those who believe" (1 Cor 1:21), because this way he respects human freedom to the utmost degree.

There is a principle, that all of you have to understand, it is called "freedom". Without freedom there is no love and God is love! Obviously freedom scandalizes us. It scandalizes us, for instance, that God allows a man to commit incest. As you know there is an enormous amount of incest in the world, an unthinkable violence. A girl terrorized by her uncle, or by her father, who rapes her at night. Why does God not intervene? How is it that God allows atrocities, constant monstrosities: the dead in Auschwitz, thousands of homicides, the wars, millions of dead, and so on?

God has wanted to save the world through the foolishness of the announcement of the Kerygma. You can close your ear to what I am saying: you are bored; you look here and there and are thinking: when will this be over? Perhaps we think that we should dominate society through politics, to make a kind of Christian *sharia*. Well, no: let the Muslims do this. The kingdom of Christ is not of this world (see Jn 18:36). As you know there is a prince in this world. The prince of this world is the devil, as St. John says (see Jn 12:31; 14:30). That is why in this world the devil always wins. Thus Nazism, communism have destroyed entire nations sowing atheism, and so forth.

Eternal Life Within Us

In this world Christ has nowhere to rest his head (see Mt 8:20) and the one who thinks that religion is for bourgeois people and limits himself to going to Mass on Sundays as a social habit is completely wrong. God has to put up with that kind of bourgeois Christianity, that social goodness of the Church that, thank God, today is in crisis and is struggling: there are no vocations; many pedophile priests have been discovered, for example. The Church is not for the sake of living better here! Even though it is true that Christians live much better than anyone else. Who can be happier than we if we live in the Kingdom? God has given us eternal life, immortal life! Is there anything greater and more marvelous than this?

God has raised our Lord Jesus, who has offered his death for every man. St. Paul says that he "was put to death for our trespasses and raised for our justification" (Rom 4:25). Christ has become man and as man he wanted to become sin for us, for all men (see 2 Cor 5:21). He suffered the punishment deserved by all who have committed incest, all those who have wrongly touched a child, who have stolen, who have defrauded, who have lied, who have committed murder.

We are giving catechesis in prisons. In several prisons in Italy, for example, there is the Way and in the community there are murderers. In Colombia there is one who has committed seventy homicides. Do you believe that he can receive forgiveness? Do you think that he can enter in a community and be full of gratitude toward God? Is it possible? Yes! Yes, it is possible! It is the truth! The Fathers of the Church say that nothing attracts the Holy Spirit more than a sinner who converts, who wants to leave sin, who wants to leave a life of misery, of evil, of iniquity.

Christ has risen for our justification. He became man; he took the place of each man. His Resurrection announces that, in him, all sins are forgiven, that he is the firstborn of a new creation, of a new reality. Someone may say: "But I am old." Well, look: new things have appeared as we have heard. What has appeared? The grace of the Holy Spirit in man that makes us children of God. St. Paul says, as we have heard, that even if we knew Christ according to the flesh, that is, exteriorly, we no longer know him like that. Now Christ lives in us with the Holy Spirit: he is in us. New things have appeared, the Holy Spirit has appeared dwelling in Christians.

Do you believe that this is only words? Well, no! I am not giving my life to make a devotional reality in the parish. I come from atheism, and I have to face young people who want the truth, not just words. Is it true that the Holy Spirit makes of us a new creation? Is it true that we have received the divine nature that dwells in us and allows us to be adopted by God as his children? I cannot adopt a dog because it does not have a human nature. God cannot adopt a man because he does not have a divine nature. In order for man to be adopted by God as his child, that man has to receive the divine nature that is given in baptism, in the Church, through the Holy Spirit.

Little by little, we are making mature communities, a serious Christian initiation, generating Christians little by little, explaining the marvels that being Christian means—being a child of God. There are whole nations, millions and millions of atheists, with very serious problems of betrayal, of selfishness, of envy, of wars, of hatred, because sin dwells in their flesh. We come from Spain, where in politics there is a terrible verbal violence, where society is decomposing at all levels: it is full of homosexual couples, the ideology of gender rules, in school they teach six-year-old children that they have to choose their own gender, decide if they want to be a man or a woman. What a horror!

We have to announce the truth! Announce Christ, risen and ascended into heaven, God has made him sit at his right hand and has constituted him *Kyrios*, above all power, virtue, domination, and he has constituted him high Priest. What does it mean? That he is eternally interceding for us. Right now Christ is before the Father interceding for us, presenting him, we could say, his wounds full of light, glorious wounds, which are a sign of his suffering for you, of the ransom he has paid for you. And why does he present them to the Father? This is the point. He presents his wounds to the Father for you!

The Letter to the Hebrews says that Christ is the splendor of the glory of God and the imprint of his substance (see Heb 1:3). The word "substance" is a philosophical word that indicates the most profound aspect, the essence of a reality. And what does it mean? "No one has ever seen God" (Jn 1:18). What is God like? What is he composed of? Well the Word of God says that Christ is the imprint of the substance of God (an imprint, for example, like the image that a ring leaves on soft wax). So that in this glorious cross that is raised up, that is presiding over our meeting, we have the imprint of the substance of God. Christ is the reflection of the glory of God.

Look at this image! The great preachers always carried the crucifix with them and they showed it to the people while they were preaching. This is very important. Scripture says: "They shall look on him whom they have pierced" (Jn 19:37). It means that in this Kerygma you have to look at the one you have pierced. Here is Christ Pantocrator. Here is Christ crucified. What shall we look at? We have to look at the imprint of the divine substance, the essence, the substance of God is this: the image of a man crucified on a cross, who has given his life for you! God is love to the sinner! In order to love you, God does not need you to be good, that you leave your lover. God has given his life for us when we were wicked (see Rom 5:8) and wanted to offer his death as a ransom for our sins.

I want to tell you again what is said about St. Jerome. He came from Dalmatia. He had a very bad temper. At the end of his life he went to live in a cave and seeing that he had to appear before the judgment of God, he would beat his chest with a stone and say: "Sinner, sinner! Hit me, because I am a sinner!" They say that once Christ appeared to him and told him: "Jerome, what will you give me?" And he answered, "Lord, what do you want me to give you? I give you my love!" And Christ remained silent. Again Christ asks: "Jerome, what will you give me?" And he answered, "My fasting, my sacrifices. For you I spend night and day scrutinizing the Scriptures and weeping for my sins." And Christ again: "Jerome, what will you give me?" Jerome did not understand anything. At the end Christ said: "Jerome, give me your sins!"

Hear this well: "Give me your sins!"

"Lord, my sins? I have been an adulterer, a lustful man. If you knew all the sins I have committed in my youth. My sins disfigure your face; they crown you with thorns; they scourge you. My lust scourges you. The robberies I have done strip you."

"Give me your sins!" Christ repeats to you, "I take them; I carry them, even if your sins crucify me, because I am love. Your sins are the destruction of love, but I want to tell you that I love you so much, so much, so much, that I am willing to go to prison for you, to suffer torture for you, to give you gratuitously not only the forgiveness but a new life, eternal life." Look how God is!

When you were baptized, the priest asked your godfather, "What do you ask of the Holy Church of God?" And your godfather replied, "Faith."

Then the priest asked, "What does faith give you?" And the godfather answered, "Eternal life." What is eternal life? Eternal life is not only happiness without end, after death. Eternal life is something that right now you either have or don't have. St. John says, "Any one who hates his brother is a murderer, and you know that no murderer has eternal life abiding in him" (1 Jn 3:15). So Christians have eternal life within them, right now. Tomorrow I can lose it if I decide not to do the will of God and make the decision that I want to sin, and that's it. The Lord lets me be free, but my baptism will be in me as if it were dead.

God has manifested his own essence. And what is this essence? To love you!

The Third Angel and the Third Dialogue: the Announcement of the Kerygma to All Present in the Meeting

Now I have to speak to you about the third angel and the third woman. On the right, there is a third dialogue. I am the angel. Angel means one who is sent and I have been sent to Sora for you. And who is the woman? You are! That is to say, there is a dialogue that I have now with you and you have to answer. The first woman answered; the second woman answered; now it is your turn. Following the example of the second woman, the Virgin Mary, you might answer, "Let it be done unto me according to what you announce! I accept it!"

What am I announcing to you? I announce to you that God has shown in Christ his essence, his nature, his most profound being. And what is his most profound being? God—Father, Son, and Holy Spirit—is love. Of what does divine love consist? In a perfect unity of the three Divine Persons. God is total love toward you, to the point that he wants to be one in you.

Is God one in you? Look at that priest: If only he were one in Christ! Who here is one with Christ as the Father and the Son are one? That is why the Book of Revelation says: "Behold, I stand at the door and knock; if any one hears my voice and opens the door, I will come in to him and eat with him, and he with me" (Rev 3:20). This means that this announcement of the Kerygma now, here in Sora, can bring you salvation, because tonight I am announcing to you the divine nature, that is, that God would like to be one with you, totally one.

But, in order to do that, you would have to give your sins to Christ: "Give me your sins!" If you give them to him, Christ will take them with him to the cross. He dies for your sins, he forgives your sins and he rises from the dead for your justification. He presents his work of salvation to the Father, because he would like you to receive the Holy Spirit now.

The Holy Spirit makes you one with the Father. As the Son and the Father are one, he makes you one with himself; he introduces you into the mystery of the Holy Trinity. What do you think about it? God wishes for all of you to leave here as true temples of the Holy Trinity, perfectly one. Do you believe that this is easy? It is not easy at all, because in order for God to be one with you, you will have to let this cross condemn you; that is, it needs to enlighten you that your life is not yet within the mystery of the Holy Trinity and that you believe that this love of God shown in Christ is the only truth.

Truth! The word *truth* is extremely important. God has created man in the truth. I go back to the first angel. God has given man preternatural gifts: one of these is the truth of the relationship of love. The truth is the relationship of love between the Father and the Son in the Holy Spirit, the relationship of love among the three Persons of the Holy Trinity. Well, original sin has broken that relationship of love that man had received.

All nature, all the beauty in nature is a relationship of love. I am an artist, a painter, and I know very well that the beauty of the trees—the roughness of the trees—sings of the smoothness of the sky. The smoothness of the sky sings of the beauty of the rocks. The rocks sing of the beauty of the river, and so on. Beauty appears only when such a relationship is given. Sirach says that God has created all things one complementing the other, because each thing should sing of the beauty of the thing next to it (see Sir 42:24–25). In the whole of creation there is a relationship of love.

It is terrible that sin has broken this truth of the relationship of love and has made mankind live in a lie. Do you live in the truth, in the truth of the relationship of love with God? Do you live totally in him, do you live a relationship of love with him or not?

When the Holy Spirit, at Pentecost, descended on the Apostles and sealed within them that the One they had seen crucified was not only the Messiah but God himself, they were stunned. A Hebrew could never have thought that a man could be God. For them God was something so transcendent they could not even pronounce the name Yahweh. Once a year the high priest would pronounce the name Yahweh after entering into the *Sancta Sanctorum*, with a chain on his feet, so that he could be pulled outside if something happened to him while he was in the presence of God. Meanwhile all the people were prostrated, face down. God is incommensurable, eternal, infinite. Who could know him?

How could a Hebrew think that that man who was crucified was God himself? That can only be testified to by the Spirit, only the Holy Spirit can seal it in the heart of man. It is such a striking news that the Apostles set out to announce it: God in person has come to earth to save all mankind! Now all mankind can be saved from death! Already now they have the possibility of not dying any more! Now men can receive the forgiveness of their sins and life immortal!

Are these only words or am I telling the truth? It is profoundly true, brothers and sisters! I speak to you in the name of the Lord. I am an angel for you. The Lord has brought me here, to Sora, so that you may listen to me, because he wants your conversion. The Desert Fathers say that from our baptism a pure water springs up and flows and it says, "Today, convert! Today, convert!" Perhaps today, after listening to this preaching, after this Word, after this announcement of the Kerygma, it would be easier for you to convert. Convert today! We Christians start each day from scratch. Convert today! This is what the Lord wants for you today.

The Lord wants your conversion today to what I am telling you. Convert to Christ and believe in the good news! What does "to convert" mean? To believe! And why don't you believe? No one can believe without the Holy Spirit. "Then, someone may think, You are contradicting yourself, Kiko. If all this is the work of the Holy Spirit, then let the Holy Spirit come and convert me!"

Have you not heard the word of St. Paul? He said: "Be attentive not to receive the grace of God in vain." Resisting the grace of the Holy Spirit is something you run the risk of doing. You are listening to me, but you do not move. God wants your life to change, but you do not want it to change. Perhaps you like to listen to me, but you do not move: you resist the grace of the Holy Spirit.

Convert and believe in the good news, in the Kerygma, in the good news, in the gospel of God! What does "to convert" mean? Christ says: "Love your enemies." Do good to those who hate you. If any one strikes you on the right cheek, turn to him the other also." If someone takes you to court to steal your house, give him also your field. If someone steals what is yours, do not claim it back. Love your enemies. Do good to those who hate you (see Mt 5:38–43).

In the Way we have told you that all this is the design of the heavenly man. God wishes us to love, that we may truly become saints, because the Holy Spirit makes us saints, because in the end we will have to give an account to God even of each word, of all we have said, of all that we have seen, of all the pornography that you have watched on television.

If you look at a woman lustfully you are already committing adultery. According to the Sermon on the Mount (see Mt 5:21–32) to commit adultery you do not need to go to bed with another man's wife; it is enough to look at a woman lustfully and you are already an adulterer, you are guilty of adultery. And to be a murderer, according to the Sermon on the Mount, you do not necessarily have to get a gun and kill someone, it is enough to detest or hate someone and thus you have already committed a homicide, you already have to answer for it in Gehenna. If you have been capable of saying of your brother or of anyone, speaking ill of him: "He is crazy", you will answer for it before the Sanhedrin. Read the Sermon on the Mount.

But the Sermon on the Mount is not a moralistic manual. No! It is a liberating work of grace! The problem that man has, after having obeyed the first angel, is that he suffers like a dog, because he lives in this lie. The one who cannot love suffers terribly. Because the truth—I pass to the second angel— is this love. A man will be happy only if he comes to love as Christ has loved us, to give himself as Christ has given himself to us. If he comes to love like this, he is happy.

That is why in the meeting in Milan, the third of last June, two thousand families stood up. Others have been sent on a mission to China and are happy. The problem of man today is not whether he has lots of money or little money. His problem is love, the truth. And the work of original sin is that it does not allow me to love. That is why, for example, there are priests that have problems with their bishop. I look for my well-being in everything. I have within me a principle that tyrannizes me, that enslaves me.

Because of this Jesus Christ does not see any man as being bad, so to speak. He sees all men as being enslaved; that is why he comes to free them with his death and Resurrection, to break their chains. Today the Lord would like you to accept the death of Christ for yourself and to say, "Lord, I would like to be a Christian! Give me your holiness. Give me your holy humility, I am willing to change. Tomorrow I will speak to my wife and to my children in a different manner. I will consider myself the last, the worst of all, as the Fathers say."

Are you willing to change, to be Christians? O holy humility of Christ! To be humble! "O holy humility of Christ," the Eastern Church says, "who can find you?" To be humble. . . . We are all proud. Free me from pride, says the Psalm. May it not dominate me. Then I will be free from grave sin! (see Ps 19:13) That is the sin of the devil. And no one can humiliate you; your daughter cannot humiliate you when she does things differently from how you think. At work you cannot be humiliated. Your husband cannot talk harshly to you, no. Sin causes that, given that we make a god of ourselves, we cannot stand anyone. Things have to be the way I think they should be, the family the way I say, work the way I say, the community the way I say. Everything as I say! And I am always resentful, always angry, because things are never as I think they should be.

"Consider yourself the last", as Silvanus of Mount Athos said—"put yourself in hell and trust in the Lord." Recognize that you should be in hell because of your sins. Be grateful to God for all he gives you. Be always happy, because you are not better than those who are in prison. Do you know what the prisons in Rome are like? Do you know how thousands of prostitutes there live? Why is it that you are not in the streets like a prostitute? Are you better than they are? "The harlots go into the kingdom of God before you" says the Lord (Mt 21:31). We are not better than anyone else. How is it possible that there are people whose lives are hell, that they have already been five times in jail, that they had been raped twice, that they have seen their fathers hit their mothers with a stick? I have lived in the shantytown, I have seen horrible things, and I have seen the suffering of the innocents. Sartre said, "Woe to the man whom the finger of God crushes against the wall!" There are people who are crushed by the sins of the others. That is the truth. Let us not be stupid bourgeois, thinking that life is something banal. No!

I am not saying this to sadden you. On the contrary! This is good news! The Lord wants to give himself to you, to enter within you, but for that you have to recognize that Christ crucified is the truth and desire to live in him, for him, with him. This that I am saying is realized if the Holy Spirit places a seal inside you and tells you: "What Kiko is saying is the truth. Courage! Go ahead!" What I announce is realized if the Holy Spirit seals it within you and you believe it.

The Holy Spirit helps you to be more humble, more holy, good, to help your wife wash the dishes, to accept your *nothingness*, to be a bit more humble. There is no Christian, there is no holiness, without humility. Tell me how humble you are and I will tell you how holy you are. That is the truth, Christ, in spite of being God, humbled himself and became man and made man he took the condition of a slave, obeying in everything until death (see Phil 2:6, 8).

To be Christian means to obey. Whom? God, who speaks to you in your history. Do not rebel; let God lead your history. "My daughter has left the Way. . . ." Patience; allow God to be the one who directs your history. Jesus Christ has let all hate him, kill him. He has trusted in the Father and from that evil God has taken our salvation:

from the greatest sin, which is to kill God, has come salvation, our salvation. O holy humility, O divine wisdom!

I conclude by saying what St. Paul says: *"Caritas Christi urget nos!"* The love of Christ urges us to think that if Christ has died for all, all have died. And he died so that man may no longer live for himself. He died so that you may no longer live for yourselves, but for him who has died and is risen for you. To live in Christ! St. Paul says: "It is no longer I who live, but Christ who lives in me" (Gal 2:20). And "whether you eat or drink, or whatever you do, do all to the glory of God" (1 Cor 10:31). To be with Christ with constant prayer: that is what monks do. It is not that they have a special spirituality, rather they underline an aspect proper to all the baptized: that God is enough, that intimacy with Christ is the only truth.

To love Christ is the only truth, the rest is vanity! Everything! And, for this love of Christ to be authentic, God allows it to be precarious and every day subjected to the temptation of the devil. St. Dominic of Sora also was tempted a thousand times with the demons of affections, with the persecutions he suffered, and so forth. He had to fight constantly, every day. That battle that he had, all of us also have. In this way God has done something very beautiful: that his love in us is something alive! God cannot stand weariness, boredom, routine, bourgeois life, tepidity. No! Christian life is something dynamic. Once Pope John Paul II told us: "You, who belong to the Neocatechumenal Way, have told all the Church that baptism is a dynamism, a way." Why do we have to be tempted? A Desert Father said, "In this life I expect nothing but temptations: temptations of old age, of sickness, of death."

The Fathers said this: "To love Christ is the only truth, the rest is vanity." Do you love Christ? St. Paul says: "If any one has no love for the Lord, let him be accursed" (1 Cor 16:22). Perhaps you say, "Kiko I do not love Christ; I love him very little." Well, this should worry you a lot.

"And what should I do, Kiko?"

Get up at night to pray; go to Mass; ask for help and say, "Lord, have pity on me, because I do not feel any love for you, I look for myself in everything, I am a disaster!" If only you were capable of saying this with your heart! Consider yourself the last, not worthy of even being in the Way, and then you will start to be in the correct way. Nothing without humility.

AN EXPERIENCE OF THE NEW EVANGELIZATION: THE *MISSIO AD GENTES*

The missio ad gentes *in Chemnitz, Germany (Formerly known as Karl Marx City).*

The *missio ad gentes* is a surprising way in which the Lord has inspired the Neocatechumenal Way to live the New Evangelization. This mission to all the nations refers to places where the gospel is not present, places where initial evangelization needs to be done. St. Paul says: "We will go to the gentiles", *ad gentes* in Latin.

We can distinguish two types of place where this evangelization is necessary: first, poor areas, where people are usually baptized, have a natural religiosity, and tend toward popular devotions; second, cities where secularization has had a huge impact and there is hardly anything left of the Catholic Church.

There are terrible places like the city of Chemnitz, in Germany, where seventy years of Communism have destroyed religion. Communists believe that religion stupefies the mind and alienates man from his primary function, which is social good and justice. Chemnitz was meant to be a model city for the Communist social order. For this reason, for example, its name was changed to Karl Marx City and a huge eleven-meter sculpture of Marx's head was placed in the city center. The diocesan Bishop says that since the fall of the Berlin Wall, what is left is a desolate city, where some 98% of the people are not baptized. It is a place where young people know nothing about Jesus Christ because they were educated by Marxists.

Confronted with the challenge of evangelizing in this city, we remembered that John Paul II had shown us the path to follow when he said "We must return to the initial apostolic model." But what does this mean? To understand it we must go back to the first years of Christianity and remember how it began to spread. Christianity, the Church, left the Cenacle to evangelize in the synagogues. After this beginning, a series of important conflicts arose that caused serious divisions, all of which we can read about in the Acts of the Apostles. These tensions began in the synagogues between those communities of Jews that had accepted Christ as the Messiah and the rest of the Jewish people, who continued to be faithful to the Torah and did not accept gentiles into their communities. The Emperor Claudius therefore considered himself obliged to expel the Jews from Rome.

In his speech to the Sixth Synod of European Bishops in 1985, John Paul II emphasized that in order to respond to the secularization of Europe, it was necessary to "return to the primary apostolic model". That means: when the first Christians had to leave the synagogues they met instead in their houses to receive instruction from the Apostles, for the breaking of bread, and to pray, as we read in the Acts of the Apostles.

In imitation of this first model, the *missio ad gentes* meets in houses in the midst of people who are not baptized. Each mission is made up of a priest and three or four families with many children; together they make present a Christian community, in the midst of pagans, a community that should produce signs that can bring forth faith: signs of love and perfect unity.

We ask the families who have already finished their neocatechumenal itinerary if they are willing to build a new community with other families. Some have nine children, some eight, some seven. They are families with older children, seventeen or eighteen years old. We ask them if they are willing to be sent in mission, for example to Chemnitz, where—as I was saying earlier—the atmosphere is totally pagan. We ask them if they think it is the will of God for them to be sent there in the manner of the "primary apostolic model". To start up the mission, they search out a place where they can meet and form the community, and the children begin to attend school. In Chemnitz, for example, the children of these families are the only Catholics in the school. As time goes on, they invite their school friends and classmates to their homes; they themselves can see how a Christian family lives.

The majority of the parents of these friends are separated, and so they are surprised to see a large family with the mother and father still together.

Once every two weeks the families go out into the streets and sing with guitars and invite the people to the catechesis; to a meeting at which Jesus Christ will be spoken of. Many people like the songs, and this makes them stop and listen and ask. Some of these passersby attend the catechesis and form communities in which the majority of the participants are not baptized. This is also happening in Almere, a city near Amsterdam, or in Amsterdam itself, in Vienna, and in Stockholm. In this way we are trying to bring people to Jesus Christ. For us the conversion of one person is worth the whole universe, because one person is worth the life of Christ. It is not a matter of great numbers, or success, but rather of saving every man.

It consoles us to see how the Holy Spirit penetrates these people when they listen to the Kerygma, the announcement of their salvation. They are enlightened; their soul is raised up and, little by little they begin to change into new people. Thus a new creation appears; a new child of God, which at first is small and needs to be sustained because it is so weak. It is all worthwhile when you see their gratitude toward us. There was an interesting case of a Hungarian intellectual, who had written various books and thanked us because, he said, he would never have gone into a church, but thanks to this type of evangelization he had met the Lord.

After some years it becomes clear that many people who were far away and pagan and had never entered a church, find a place in these Christian communities and begin an itinerary of conversion or a return to the faith. These communities, that do not begin in a sacred building, but rather live in the midst of the world, constitute a real "court of the gentiles" in which men can get close to God, as Benedict XVI indicated.

This does not mean that we want to be a substitute for parishes; quite the opposite. It is simply a way of creating new parishes in areas that are totally atheist. Sometimes, thanks to a *missio ad gentes*, new communities begin to appear, so much so that the place where they are meeting is no longer sufficient. Then a church with a new aesthetic needs to be built, a parish that can be a *domus ecclesiae;* a place where the Church gathers and that has a *catechumenium* where each small community can have its own small room in which the members can meet to listen to the Word of God.

In this way we are initiating a new evangelization in the big, secularized cities of Europe, America, Oceania, and so on—a new way of doing it. And when we go to places that are more religious, we go with a different plan, more suited to the reality of the place.

NEW SIGNS FOR MODERN MAN

There are places in the world where man has lost the sense of the sacred, of the religious; this is partly due to recent social movement, nihilism, modern philosophies, and wars. Today man no longer turns to God when facing illness, as he once did. For these reasons nowadays, to evangelize in some places it is impossible to begin with religious signs and symbols, as you would find in a cathedral, for example. Some people are so secularized and so prejudiced against anything religious that they will never go into a church.

In the Way we have seen the need for finding new signs that can break through to this modern and secularized man who doesn't even live according to the traditional model of the Judeo-Christian family. We have had to think again about how to approach this new man.

Communism reached out to modern man through social justice, and many people followed. The Church also became involved with social work, but modern man is not even interested in social work anymore. The old ideologies have fallen from grace, along with the utopias and social movements, and man has been left in a state of disillusionment and despondency that in the end leads many people to suicide, alcoholism, for example. In short; social breakdown and desperation are widespread. This situation is most evident in young people and women in the cities and capitals of the world. How many women are alone in the world's major cities?

When the Way arrives in a parish, the first thing that is done is to discuss with the pastor how it is necessary to move from a pastoral ministry of sacramentalization to a pastoral ministry of evangelization for those who find themselves outside the Church. We say that what we can take to people who are interested in the Church is what Jesus Christ says: "Love one another as I have loved you." It is about a new dimension of love, an astonishing love. Christ loved us when we were his enemies and because of this in the Sermon on the Mount he says: "Love your enemies" (Mt 5:44) and later "That they may all be one . . . so that the world may believe" (Jn 17:21).

But loving in this dimension is difficult when you are in a crowd, because you cannot love others unless you know them. The Christian community cannot be an anonymous crowd, because if it is, then it cannot give concrete signs of love.

For example, if I ask someone to write down the names of all his friends, (names, place of work, and home address), he will not be able to recall more than thirty, because our capacity for really knowing, having a true relationship with another, is finite. Thus, if we want to establish a Christian community that can give tangible, visible signs of love—either in the dimension of love for the enemy or perfect unity—such a community cannot be too large.

We know that the early Church communities were small, and they met in houses. In Scripture we read that St. Paul greeted the Church that met in the house of Ninphas. It is not a simple question of numbers, but of quality and profound content.

The Way is immersed in this work: how to make a Christian community—various brothers that form a group and attend catechesis guided by catechists—go through the stages of their baptism, renewing it step-by-step until their faith matures; until they can love the enemy. We want these people to discover that their baptism is dynamic, a way, a march toward the Promised Land, toward the real city, which is the heavenly Jerusalem. On this march, helped by the Holy Spirit, we must understand that we need to reach a new level of faith. The Letter to the Ephesians says this: that God, ascending to the heavens, bestowed gifts upon men and some he made apostles, others evangelists, others teachers, to some he gave the gift of service, the gift of miracles, the gift of tongues, among others, and that all these gifts come from the Holy Spirit to grow up in every way into him who is the head. Without these gifts, these charisms, our faith would remain impoverished and small. This is not just about having a bricks-and-mortar church and getting people to go to Mass. It is much deeper. This is what the Neocatechumenal Way is trying to achieve inside and outside the parish.

THE TRANSMISSION OF FAITH TO CHILDREN AND LOVE FOR THE ENEMY

In this Christian initiation that is called the Way, being open to life is fundamental. Pope Paul VI clearly stated in *Humanae Vitae* that "every conjugal act must be open to life." Incredibly, the people in the Way believe and obey these words.

We explain to the families that there are three altars:

First is the altar of the holy Eucharist, where Christ offers himself as a sacrifice for us and gives us his divine and glorious Body; through eating his Flesh and drinking his Blood divine life is nourished in us.

The second altar is the nuptial bed, where the marriage becomes a sacrament, an image of the love of Christ for his Church. The spouses always pray to God before celebrating the conjugal act; they kneel down and ask the Lord to be present, always keeping in mind that the body is worthy of honor and glory. They know that to cooperate with God in giving life to a new human being is something immense, because a person may appear who didn't exist before but who will now exist for all eternity. Whether or not to have a child is a hugely important question. Because of this, the Church has always seen children as a gift from God, a blessing, as referred to in the Psalms and rest of the Old Testament.

The third altar is the table where the family eats and receives food from God. We encourage the whole family to eat together—parents and children gathered around the table. This is the same table around which they are also taught to pass on the Faith through a domestic celebration every Sunday, the day of the Lord. In this Sunday liturgy faith is transmitted to the children and Scripture is made present, relevant, and real. The family listens to a passage of Scripture, it could be from a Gospel or another reading from the Old or New Testaments, and then the parents ask the children how this word enlightens their lives. The parents ask about problems the children are having at school, at university, with their brothers and sisters, or within themselves. Our experience of this liturgy is wonderful because families are really finding it a way of encountering the Lord. In the Way there are many large families whose children are all in the Church. Through this home liturgy the children can be helped in facing a society that is hostile to the values and the reality of Eternal Life that is the gospel.

THE GREATEST THING FOR A CHRISTIAN

To conclude I would like to emphasize that, written like this, everything seems easy, but the evangelization always takes place amid difficulties. We have been persecuted and expelled from many parishes. Sometimes the Way is misunderstood and confused with a sect. However, we want to follow Jesus Christ and walk in his footsteps, and we know that persecution is the source of true success, that persecution aids conversion. Anything that makes us more similar to Jesus Christ is the truth and there is nothing greater for a Christian than to be similar to Christ, crucified, hated, persecuted; and the more good he did the more they wanted to kill him. This is why Christians, together with Christ, do not have anywhere to lay their head in this world.

Our true city is the heavenly homeland, where we hope to go soon. But while the Lord has us here he invites us to participate in his mission of love. Nothing greater exists than to love as he loved us; to participate in the very essence of God, which is to love the other even when the other is evil and is our enemy. This is what it means to participate in his glory.

St. Paul says "For we are [God's] workmanship, created in Christ Jesus for good works, which God prepared beforehand, that we should walk in them" (Eph 2:10).

~